China
The Country And
The People

Published by: The Commercial Press (U.S.) Ltd.
13-17 Elizabeth Street, 2nd Floor
New York, NY 10013

China: the Country and the People
Intermediate-Advanced READ ABOUT CHINA

Editor: Rachel Feng

Printed in Hong Kong

http://www.chinese4fun.net

Contents
目 录

PUBLISHER'S NOTE

After studying one to two years of Chinese you have also gained the knowledge of quite a bit of vocabulary. You may be wondering whether there are any other ways for you to further improve your Chinese language proficiency? Although there are a lot of books in the market that are written for people who are studying Chinese it is not easy to find an interesting and easy to read book that matches up to one's level of proficiency. You may find the content and the choice of words for some books to be too difficult to handle. You may also find some books to be too easy and the content is too naive for high school students and adults. Seeing the demand for this kind of learning materials we have designed a series of reading materials, which are composed of vivid and interesting content, presented in a multi-facet format. We think this can help students who are learning Chinese to solve the above problems. Through our reading series you can improve your Chinese and at the same time you will learn a lot of China culture.

Our series includes Chinese culture, social aspects of China, famous Chinese literary excerpts, pictorial symbols of

China, famous Chinese heroes...and many other indispensable aspects of China for those who want to really understand Chinese culture. While enjoying the reading materials one can further one's knowledge of Chinese culture from different angles. The content of the series are contextualized according to the wordbase categorization of HSK. We have selected our diction from the pre-intermediate, intermediate to advanced level of Chinese language learners. Our series is suitable for students at the pre-intermediate, intermediate to advanced level of Chinese and working people who are studying Chinese on their own.

The body of our series is composed of literary articles. The terms used in each article are illustrated with the romanised system called Hànyǔ pīnyīn for the ease in learning the pronunciation. Each article has an English translation with explanation of the vocabulary. Moreover there is related background knowledge in Expansion Reading. Interesting games are added to make it fun to learn. We aim at presenting a three-dimensional study experience of learning Chinese for our readers.

Zhōngguó zài nǎli

中国在哪里?

shì zěnyàng de dìfang

是怎样的地方?

Where is China? What Kind of the Place is it?

Pre-reading Questions

1. Do you know where is China? In terms of area which is the bigger one? China or the U.S.A.?

2. When you are traveling in China will you encounter the problem of time difference because of the various time zones?

3. The U.S.A. has a population of over 300 millions but do you know what is the population of China?

Zhōngguó de dìlǐ huánjìng

❶ 中国 的 地理 环境

Cóng shìjiè dìtú lái kàn, kěyǐ jiàn dào Zhōngguó
从 世界 地图 来 看, 可以 见 到 中国

zài Yàzhōu dàlù de zuì dōng bù Yīnwèi Zhōngguó de dōngmiàn
在 亚洲 大陆[1] 的 最 东 部。因为 中国 的 东面

hé nánmiàn miànduì dà hǎiyáng xīmiàn hé běimiàn bèi shāmò
和 南面 面对 大 海洋, 西面 和 北面 被 沙漠[2]

hé gāoyuán bāowéi Zhège wèizhi yīfāngmiàn lìng gǔdài
和 高原[3] 包围。这个 位置 一方面 令 古代

Zhōngguó yào huā qìlì cái néng jiēchù qítā wénmíng dìqū
中国 要 花 气力 才 能 接触[4]其他 文明 地区,

中国

lìngyīfāngmiàn　　yě　ràng　Zhōngguó　bǐjiào　shǎo　duìwài　zhànzhēng
另一方面 也 让 中国 比较 少 对外 战争，

kěyǐ　ānwěn　de　fāzhǎn
可以 安稳[5]地 发展。

Jīntiān Zhōngguó de miànjī yǒu　　　wàn píngfānggōnglǐ
今天 中国 的 面积 有 960 万 平方公里，

gēn Ōuzhōu huòzhě Měiguó chàbuduō Zài dìtú shang kàn
跟 欧洲 或者 美国 差不多。在 地图 上 看，

Zhōngguó xiàng yī kuài yèzi Cóng dìshì lái kàn zhè kuài
中国 像 一 块 叶子。从 地势[6]来 看，这 块

yèzi shì qīngxié de xībian gāo dōngbian dī jiù xiàng
叶子 是 倾斜[7]的，西边 高，东边 低，就 像

阶梯[8]一样。最高一级的阶梯是西部的青藏高原，向来有"世界屋脊[9]"之称，平均海拔[10]4,000米以上。第二阶梯低一点，平均海拔1,000至2,000米。可是在第二阶梯上，也有中国最低的盆地[11]，比海要低155米。第三阶梯在1,000米以下，向东直达太平洋，主要是平原[12]和丘陵[13]。在第三阶梯从北向南分布着三个大平原，土地肥沃[14]，是中国重要的农业区。

中国著名的神话故事——女娲补天，就是以这种由西斜向东的地势做背景。

GLOSSARY

1	大陆	continent	2	沙漠	desert
3	高原	plateaus	4	接触	get in contact with
5	安稳	steady	6	地势	natural relief
7	倾斜	tilting	8	阶梯	ladder
9	脊	ridge	10	海拔	sea level
11	盆地	basin	12	平原	plains
13	丘陵	hills	14	肥沃	fertile

Translation

❶ The Geography and the Environments of China

From the world map, China is located on the eastern most part of the Asian continent. The location is due to the fact that China is facing deep oceans to her east and south while she is surrounded by deserts and plateaus in the west and north. China had to make great efforts to get in contact with other civilized regions with such a location; however, this also meant she had steady development over the centuries without much involvement in foreign wars.

Today, China measures 960,000,000 km^2 in area, similar to Europe or the US. The shape of China on a map can be compared to the shape of a leaf. From the perspective of topography, this leaf resembles a ladder, tilting from the high west to the low east. The highest point of the ladder in the west lies on the Qinghai-Tibetan Plateau (Qingzang Plateau) which is known as "the ridge of the roof of the world". The elevated area is over 4,000m above sea level. The second part of the ladder is a bit lower at 1,000 to 2,000m on average above sea level. Nevertheless, the lowest basin of China was discovered here and is recorded at 155m below sea level. The third part of ladder is below 1,000m and consists mainly of plains and hills stretching east towards the Pacific Ocean. Three vast plains here, ranging from the north to the south, are rich in fertile soil and are the major agricultural regions in China.

The famous Chinese myth of "Nüwa Mended the Sky" was set in the context of such a tilted natural relief from the west to the east.

❷ 中国 的 概况

Yóuyú Zhōngguó de dìshì xiàng dōng qīngxié Zhōngguó zuì
由于 中国 的 地势 向 东 倾斜，中国 最

cháng de sì tiáo hé dōu shì xiàng dōng liú de Dì yī dà
长 的 四 条 河 都 是 向 东 流 的。第 一 大

hé shì Chángjiāng cháng gōnglǐ Chángjiāng yěshì shìjiè dì
河 是 长江，长 6,300 公里。长江 也是 世界 第

sān dà hé Chángjiāng zài Zhōngguó de zhōngjiān Zhōngguó rén shuō
三 大 河。长江 在 中国 的 中间，中国 人 说

nánfāng hé běifāng shì yǐ Chángjiāng wéi jièxiàn de Zhōngguó
南方 和 北方，是 以 长江 为 界线 的。中国

de dì èr dà hé shì Huánghé cháng gōnglǐ Huánghé
的 第 二 大 河 是 黄河，长 5,500 公里。黄河

shì yǐngxiǎng wénmíng de zhòngyào héliú
是 影响[1]文明 的 重要 河流。

Yóuyú tiānrán héliú dà duō shì yóu xī wǎng dōng liú
由于 天然 河流 大多 是 由 西 往 东 流

de suǒyǐ gǔdài Zhōngguó rén kāizáo le nán běi xiàng de
的，所以 古代 中国 人 开凿[15]了 南 北 向 的

dà yùnhé Zhè shì shìjiè zuì cháng de yùnhé tā de
大 运河[16]。这 是 世界 最 长 的 运河，它 的

lìshǐ yě hěn cháng shì yǔ Chángchéng qí míng de wěidà
历史 也 很 长，是 与 长城 齐名[17]的 伟大

gōngchéng
工程。

The Tiger-leaping Gorge of
the Yangtze River

中国 的 面积 大，地形[18] 又 复杂，所以 气候 也 有 很 多 变化。中国 从 南 到 北，跨 了 纬度[19] 接近 50 度，从 热带[20] 到 寒温带[21] 气候 都 有。从 东 到 西，又 跨 了 经度[22] 60 多 度，东部 受 海洋 的 季风[23] 影响[24]，西部 离 海洋 很 远，是 大陆 型 气候。虽然 中国 跨 了 五 个 时区[25]，但是 全国 的 时间 是 统一 的。

北京 是 中国 的 首都。北京 也是 中国 最后 三 个 王朝 的 首都。上海 是 中国 最 大 城市，也是 经济 中心。中国 最 大 的 地方 行政 单位 是 省，省 的 政治 中心 叫做 省会[26]。有些 省 住 了 很 多 少数民族[27]，这些 省 叫做 自治区[28]。

GLOSSARY

15	开凿	build	
16	运河	canal	
17	齐名	as well known as	
18	地形	terrain	
19	纬度	latitude	
20	热带	tropical	

21 寒温带 cold temperate climates   22 经度 longitude
23 季风 monsoon   24 影响 be influenced by
25 时区 time zone   26 省会 provincial capital
27 少数民族 national minority   28 自治区 autonomous regions

Translation

❷ A Profile of China

As China is tilted towards the east, the four longest rivers also flow in the same direction. The Yangtze River (Changjiang) ranks the first with a length of 6,300km. It is the third longest river in the world. The Yangtze River is in the middle of China. It divides the whole country into Northern China and Southern China. The second longest is the Yellow River (Huanghe) which is 5,500km long. The Chinese civilization has been strongly influenced by the Yellow River.

As the natural rivers generally run from west to east, the Chinese built a large canal, The Grand Canal, running from north to south in the past. This was the longest canal in the ancient world. This project was also as well known as the Great Wall.

The climate of China varies greatly due to the vast area and the complex terrain. From the south to the north, China stretches over the continent for about 50 degrees in latitude. So, she experiences varying weather conditions from tropical to cold temperate climates. From the east to the west, she stretches about 60 degrees or more in longitude. The east is under the influence of the ocean monsoons while the west, being far away from the sea, has a continental climate. Though China covers five time zones, there is no time difference throughout the country.

Beijing is the capital of China. She was also the capital of the last three dynasties in China. Being the largest city, Shanghai is also the economic hub of China. The largest unit of local administration is the province. (This is similar to a state in the US.) The political centre of a province is called the provincial capital. Some provinces which are highly populated by national minorities are called autonomous regions.

❸ 中国 的 自然 和 人文 风景

由于 中国 的 地势 复杂，历史 又 长，

所以 中国 的 自然 风景 和 人文[29] 风景 都 很

美丽。中国 最 高 的 山峰 是 珠穆朗玛 峰[30]，

在 青藏 高原 上，是 世界 第 一 高峰[31]。除了

珠穆朗玛 峰，中国 还 有 很 多 雪山。中国 最

美丽 的 山 是 黄山，虽然 不 是 很 高，但是

山峰 很 多，山 势 也 很 特别，看 起来 像

一 幅 变化万千[33] 的 中国 山水 画。在 中国

的 东部 和 西部，分别 有 两 座 山，被 古代

中国人 认为 是 神 山。东部 的 一 座 叫做

泰 山，是 看 日出 的 好 地方。中国 的 第 一

个 皇帝 曾经 上 泰 山，表示 自己 做 皇帝，

是 得到 天 的 帮助。西部 的 叫做 昆仑 山，

中国人 认为 它 是 天 和 地 的 通道[34]，有 很

多 神 住 在 昆仑 山。中国 的 海岸线[35] 也 很

The Terra-Cotta Warriors guarding the tomb of Qinshihuang — the clay figures of warriors and horses buried with the dead

cháng yǒu hěn duō měilì de hǎijǐng hé hǎitān
长，有很多美丽的海景和海滩。

Yóuyú lìshǐ cháng Zhōngguó yǒu hěn duō gǔdū lìrú
由于历史长，中国有很多古都[36]，例如

Xī'ān Nánjīng Hángzhōu Xī'ān shì shí liù gè wángcháo
西安、南京、杭州。西安是十六个王朝

de shǒudū Zhōngguó dì yī gè huángdì yě yǐ Xī'ān
的首都，中国第一个皇帝也以西安

zuò shǒudū shìjiè zhùmíng de bīngmǎyǒng jiù shì zài
做首都，世界著名的兵马俑[37]就是在

Xī'ān
西安。

GLOSSARY

29 人文　artificial
31 高峰　the highest mountain
33 变化万千　ever-changing
35 海岸线　coastline
37 兵马俑　the Terracotta Army

30 珠穆朗玛峰　Mount Everest
32 看起来　look like
34 通道　passage
36 古都　old capital

Translation

❸ The Natural Scenery and the Artificial Scenery of China

Due to her irregular physical relief and long-standing history, both natural and artificial sceneries are so fascinating in China. Mount Everest on the Tibetan Plateau is the highest mountain in China which ranks first in the world. Other than this, China also has many snow-covered mountains. The most beautiful mountain is the Yellow Mountain (Huangshan). It is not very high but it has a lot of peaks. The mountainous relief is so spectacular that it looks like an ever-changing Chinese landscape painting. To the east and west, there were once two mountains crowned with the title, "Mountains of God". In the east lies Mount Tai, offering the best place to view a sunrise. The first emperor in Chinese history once visited Mount Tai to declare that he had received the mandate of heaven (this is the right to rule). The Kunlun Mountains run westward and traditionally the Chinese have seen them as a passage between the heaven and the earth where many goddesses stay. Further, China's coastline is notably long, thus embracing many enchanting views and beaches by the sea.

Because of her long history, China has many old capitals, for instance, Xi'an, Nanking and Hanzhou. Xi'an was once the capital for 16 dynasties. When we go back in Chinese history, the first emperor also founded his capital at Xi'an. The renowned world heritage site of the Terracotta Army is found there.

❹ 中国 的 人口

中国 的 人口 超过 十 三 亿，是 世界
上 人口 最 多 的 国家。虽然 中国 经过 很
多 战争，但是 因为 农业 发达，不断 改良[38]
技术，引入 新 的 农作物[39]，所以 人口 一直
很 多。在 中国 种 米，每年 可以 收成[40] 两 三
次。美洲 的 玉米、马铃薯[41]、甘薯[42] 传 到 中国，
因为 很 容易 种植，很 多 地方 种，于是 可以
养 更 多 人口。

近 二 百 年，中国 人 口 太 多，又 受
外国 入侵，变 得 很 贫穷[43]。但是 第 二 次 世界
大战 的 时候，
中国 和 日本
作战，中国 人口
仍然 有 四 亿
五 千 万 人。

The crowded cities

Hòulái zhànzhēng jiéshù Zhōngguó bǐjiào āndìng jiāshang
后来 战争 结束，中国 比较 安定⁴⁴，加上

zhèngfǔ gǔlì rénkǒu bùduàn zēngjiā Jīngguò niándài
政府 鼓励⁴⁵，人口 不断 增加。经过 1960 年代

de jīhuāng hé Wénhuàdàgémìng yě méiyǒu jiǎnshǎo hěn duō
的 饥荒⁴⁶ 和 文化大革命，也 没有 减少 很 多

rénkǒu nián Wénhuàdàgémìng jiéshù shí Zhōngguó yǒu
人口。1976 年 文化大革命 结束 时，中国 有

shí yì rén Yóuyú rénkǒu zēngjiā tài duō suǒyǐ Zhōngguó
十 亿 人。由于 人口 增加 太 多，所以 中国

cǎiqǔ le hěn duō kòngzhì rénkǒu de cuòshī
采取 了 很 多 控制 人口 的 措施。

GLOSSARY

38 改良	improve	39 农作物	crop	40 收成	reap a harvest
41 马铃薯	potato	42 甘薯	sweet potato	43 贫穷	poor
44 安定	stable	45 鼓励	encouragement	46 饥荒	famine

Translation

❹ The Population of China

China has the highest population in the world of over 1.3 billion people. Despite many wars, thanks to the developed agriculture and continually improved technology to introduce new crops, the population of China has been remarkably high. Growing rice may reap a harvest two or three times a year. The imports of corn, potatoes and sweet potatoes from the United States are able to feed the growing number of people. These foods are easily grown and thus they are also popular in farms. In the recent two hundred years, China has become rather poor because of overpopulation problems and foreign invasion. Nevertheless, during World War II when China fought against Japan, she still recorded 450,000,000 people.

After the war, China became more stable than before. With the encouragement of the government, the population began to increase. In spite of the 1960's famines and the Cultural Revolution, China's population did not go down by much. In 1976, the Cultural Revolution came to an end. There were one billion people in China. Since the population had grown too fast, China has adopted a series of birth control measures.

Expansion Reading

Why is the Yellow River (Huanghe) yellow?

Since the Yellow River's water is yellow, China has a proverb saying that it is helpless to wash away your mark with the Yellow River's water when you have done something wrong. The silt carrying capacity of the Huanghe is the largest in the world. The average silt content is 35 kg/m^3, which once amounted to 920 kg/m^3 in 1977, since the middle course of the River runs through the Loess Plateau. The Plateau is measured between 1,000 to 1,500m above sea level. This is a huge area of loose loess of about 400,000 km^2 in area. Since the silt carrying capacity is great and the river flow in the lower course decreases, the silt deposits in the river continually lead to the elevation of the riverbeds. In some places, the riverbeds are even higher than the land. The lower course of the Huanghe is usually hit by floods and thus it has shifted the direction of flow from time to time. To manage the Huanghe has long been a serious problem for China. Four thousand years ago, a king called Da Yu (大禹, Yu the Great) who tamed the raging waters regardless of the difficulties, gained great respect from the Chinese people.

The second largest river of China — The Yellow River

GAMES FOR FUN

The following is a map of China. Find the locations of Beijing, Shanghai, Hong Kong, Taiwan, the Yellow River and the Yangtze River appropriately.

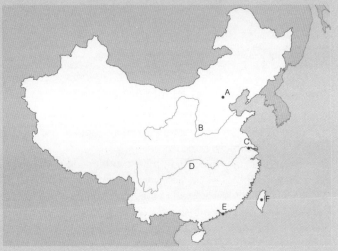

The Map of China

1. Beijing _____

2. Hong Kong _____

3. Shanghai _____

4. Taiwan _____

5. the Yellow River _____

6. the Yangtze River _____

Wénmíng gǔ guó de lìshǐ

文明古国的历史

The History of an Ancient Civilized State

Pre-reading Questions

1. Among the Four Ancient Countries of Magnificent Civilizations does China have the shortest or the longest history?

2. Who was the first person started building the Great Wall of China?

Wénmíng gǔ guó de zǎoqī

❶ 文明 古 国 的 早期[1]

Shìjiè yǒu sì dà wénmíng gǔ guó Zhōngguó shì
世界 有 四 大 文 明 古 国， 中 国 是

qízhōng yī gè Zhōngguó rén yě shuō bù qīngchu Zhōngguó
其中 一 个。 中 国 人 也 说 不 清 楚 中 国

lìshǐ yǒu duō cháng Rúguǒ
历史 有 多 长。 如果

cóng Zhōngguó yǒu cháodài kāishǐ
从 中 国 有 朝代[2] 开始

jìsuàn Zhōngguó zhǐ sān
计算， 中 国 只 三

qiān liù bǎi nián lìshǐ
千 六 百 年 历史。

The colorful flower-patterned pottery of the Yang Shao Culture

可是 中国 有 朝代 之前，传说 有 一 个
黄帝，他 是 中国 人 的 祖先，所以 中国 人
叫 自己 做 黄帝 子孙。如果 从 黄帝 开始
计算，中国 就 有 五 千 年 历史 了。

到底 有 没有 黄帝 呢？从 地下 掘
出来 的 东西 看，中国 在 很 早 以前，沿 着
黄河 和 长江，甚至 比 黄河 更 北 的 地方，
已经 有 很 多 小 国，有 很 长期[3] 的 活动。

现在 发现 了 一 万 年 前 种 的 米，八 千
年 前 做 的 漆器[4]、木 房子，还 有 五 六 千
年 前 祭 神[5] 的 地方。有些 祭 神 的 地方 大
到 不 容易 被 人 找 到，因为 在 它 上面，
现在 竟然[6] 有 几 条 村子[7]，住 了 很 多 人。
大家 以为 那 块 地 本来 就 是 高 的，从来
没有 想 过 那 是 几 千 年 前 由 人 做
出来 的。

16

Suǒyǐ	Zhōngguó	de	lìshǐ	yǒu	duō	cháng	yào	děng	cóng
所以	中国	的	历史	有	多	长	，要	等	从

dìxià	zhǎo	dào	gèng	duō	dōngxi	cáinéng	gòu	shuō	de	qīngchu
地下	找	到	更	多	东西	，才能	够	说	得	清楚 。

GLOSSARY

1 早期 early stage   2 朝代 dynasty
3 长期 long-term   4 漆器 lacquerware; lacquer work
5 祭神 offer a sacrifice to God   6 竟然 unexpectedly
7 村子 village

Translation

❶ The Early Stage of an Ancient Country of a Magnificent Civilization

There are four ancient countries with magnificent civilizations and China is one of them. Even the Chinese themselves are not sure how long Chinese history is. In terms of kingdoms and dynasties, China only has 3,600 years of history. According to legend, it was believed that Yellow Emperor (Huangdi) was the ancestor of the Chinese before the start of the kingdoms and dynasties. So, the Chinese regard themselves as the descendants of Yellow Emperor. Starting from Yellow Emperor, China has 5,000 years of history.

However, did Yellow Emperor really exist in the past? By observing the things unearthed from the ground, many tribes once had long-term activities along the Yangtze River, the Yellow River or even further north of China. At present, we have discovered rice paddies grown ten thousand years ago, lacquerware and wooden huts with eight thousand years of history, and even sacred places for their gods from five to six thousand years before. Some sacred places were so big that it is not easy to locate them. And now, some villages are still highly populated. What people see as a natural highland, surprisingly, was carved out by human hands a few thousand years ago.

So we can be more definite about the history of China only after digging up more things in the ground.

❷ 中国 的 皇帝

中国 第 一 个 皇帝 叫做 秦始皇。在
他 之前，中国 已经 有 王。秦始皇 想要
一 个 更 伟大[8] 的 名字，他 把 "皇" 字，
加 上 传说 的 中国 祖先 黄帝 的 "帝" 字，
合 起来 叫做 "皇帝"。秦始皇 很 有 现代
编号[9] 的 观念[10]，他 是 第 一 个 皇帝，所以

Qinshihuang

叫做 始皇帝。他
以后 的 皇帝，
就 叫做 二 世、三
世。不过 他 的
愿望 没有 实现，
秦朝 没有 三 世
皇帝。

秦始皇 决定 不
让 他 的 亲戚[11]，

即 贵族 来 管理 政府。贵族 可以 生活 得 很 好，但是 在 政府 里 没有 工作。贵族 就 像 一 间 家族 公司 的 小 股东[12]，皇帝 就 像 是 大 股东。大 股东 找 有 能力 的 人 来 管理 公司，这 些 人 叫做 官员。很 多 官员 本来 是 老百姓。皇帝 这个 大 股东 爱 自己 做 行政 总裁。不过，有时 贵族 还是 不 守 规矩[13]，想 管理 这个 "家族[14] 公司"。

中国 也 有 老百姓[15] 做 皇帝。汉朝（公元 前 206 年 至 公元 220 年）的 开国 皇帝[16] 是 第 一 个 当 上 皇帝 的 老百姓。他 最初 完全 不 知道 要 在 政府 里 讲 礼仪[17]，还 要 人 教 他 才 知道 皇帝 是 怎样 做 的。

GLOSSARY

8	伟大	great	9	编号	number
10	观念	sense, concept			
11	亲戚	relative	12	股东	shareholder
13	规矩	rules of a community or organization			
14	家族	family	15	老百姓	ordinary people
16	开国皇帝	the emperor of founding a state			
17	礼仪	etiquette			

Translation

❷ The Emperors of China

The first emperor in historic China was called Qinshihuang. Before him, China had already had many kings. To secure a more honorable title, Qin coined a new term for emperor (皇帝, huangdi), by combining the titles of *huang* (皇, emperor) and *di* (帝, emperor). This new term was homophonic with the name of the "Yellow Emperor", the ancestor of the Chinese. Qin had a good sense of the modern number system. He was the first emperor and thus he crowned himself *Shihuangdi* (始皇帝, the first emperor). His successors were named *Qinershi* (秦二世) and *Qinsanshi* (秦三世) (literally meaning the Second Emperor and the Third Emperor of the Qin Dynasty respectively). Nevertheless, his dream was not fulfilled. The Qin Dynasty came to an end after the second emperor.

Qinshihuang made up his mind not to employ his relatives or the nobility to administer the government. The nobility could still live well though they had no job in the government. The nobility was just like a family business's minor shareholders, while the emperor was the major stockholder. The major stockholder hired capable men who were mainly commoners as officials to work for the government, and was himself the CEO. Sometimes, the nobility did not follow the rules and made attempts to manage the family business.

In Chinese history, there were commoners who became emperors. The first emperor of the Han Dynasty (206 BC — 220 AD) was originally a commoner with a humble background. He was even not aware of the etiquette performed in the government and had to ask someone to teach him how to behave like a king.

❸ 近代 的 中国
Jìndài de Zhōngguó

由 秦始皇 到 最后
Yóu Qínshǐhuáng dào zuìhòu

一 个 皇帝，经过 了 二
yī gè huángdì jīngguò le èr

千 年。1911 年 中国 发生
qiān nián nián Zhōngguó fāshēng

革命[18]，也 学习 西方，不要
gémìng yě xuéxí xīfāng bùyào

皇帝，变 成 民 国，也 叫做
huángdì biàn chéng mín guó yě jiàozuò

共和国。领导[19] 革命 的 人
gònghéguó Lǐngdǎo gémìng de rén

Sun Yat-sen (Sun Zhongshan)

叫做 孙 中山，曾经 在 香港 读书，在 美国
jiàozuò Sūn Zhōngshān céngjīng zài Xiānggǎng dúshū zài Měiguó

生活。1912 年，中华 民 国 成立。这样，中国
shēnghuó nián Zhōnghuá mín guó chénglì Zhèyàng Zhōngguó

也 有 了 政党[20]、国会[21]。
yě yǒu le zhèngdǎng guóhuì

没有 皇帝 的 中国 最初 并 不 是 很
Méiyǒu huángdì de Zhōngguó zuìchū bìng bù shì hěn

顺利。1911 年 中国 已经 很 穷。没有 皇帝
shùnlì nián Zhōngguó yǐjing hěn qióng Méiyǒu huángdì

之后，很 多 军人 想 控制 政府，于是 不 停
zhīhòu hěn duō jūnrén xiǎng kòngzhì zhèngfǔ yúshì bù tíng

打仗，又 向 外国 借 钱 买 武器。这 时候，
dǎzhàng yòu xiàng wàiguó jiè qián mǎi wǔqì Zhè shíhou

日本 趁机[22] 入侵[23]。最后 中国 和 日本 打 了
Rìběn chènjī rùqīn Zuìhòu Zhōngguó hé Rìběn dǎ le

一 场 八 年 的 战争，直到 第 二 次 世界
yī chǎng bā nián de zhànzhēng zhídào dì èr cì shìjiè

大战²⁴ 结束 为止。没有 想 到，抗日 战争²⁵
刚刚 结束，中国 又 发生 内战²⁶。最后 国民党²⁷
的 军队 被 打败，退 到 台湾。共产党 建立
了 中华人民 共和国，领导 人 是 毛 泽东。

毛 泽东 认为 中国人 头脑²⁸
里 仍然 有 很 多 旧 东西，
所以 要 有 文化大革命²⁹。这 场
十 年 的 文化大革命，直到
1976 年 毛 泽东 去世 才 结束。
文化大革命 之后，邓 小平 提倡³⁰
改革，提倡 开放 中国，引起 最近 三 十 年
中国 的 大 变化。

The leader of the Chinese Communist Party, The first chairman of the People's Republic of China — Mao Zedong

GLOSSARY

18 革命 revolution   19 领导 lead   20 政党 political party
21 国会 Congress   22 趁机 take advantage of the occasion
23 入侵 invade   24 第二次世界大战 the World War II
25 抗日战争 the War of Resistance against Japan   26 内战 Civil war
27 国民党 the Kuomintang   28 头脑 brains, mind
29 文化大革命 Cultural Revolution   30 提倡 advocate

Translation

❸ The China in Recent History

There were 2,000 years from Qinshihuang to the last emperor. After the 1911 Revolution, modeled on the West, China overthrew the monarchy and set up a republic called the People's Republic of China. She then started to have political parties and a congress. The leader of the revolution was Dr. Sun Yat-sen. He once studied in Hong Kong and had lived in the United States.

At first, it was a hard time for China without an emperor. In 1911 China was very poor. Due to the absence of the emperor, many warlords wanted to take control of the government. Therefore, wars became inevitable and these warlords even borrowed loans from abroad for buying weapons. Taking full advantage at that time, Japan invaded China. Both countries entered into war for eight years until the end of World War II. No one could predict that this would be immediately followed by a civil war in China. At last, the Kuomintang (国民党, KMT) was defeated and they retreated to Taiwan. The Communist Party set up the People's Republic of China (PRC) with Mao Zedong as the leader.

Mao thought that the Chinese still could not get rid of traditional thinking. So, a cultural revolution was necessary. The Cultural Revolution lasted for ten years totally and came to an end with the death of Mao in 1976. After this, Deng Xiaoping introduced a series of reforms to open the country which has brought tremendous changes to China in the recent 30 years.

The First Emperor of China — Qinshihuang

Qinshihuang was the first emperor who unified China. Unlike the previous kings, he neither allowed relatives to administer the country nor granted any lands to the nobility. Instead, he founded an official system to appoint officials to manage the government, ranging from the regional to the central levels. In this way his decrees could be sent to any place in the country. This was different from the previous kings when the whole country was broken up into many feudal states, which made it possible for the people not to follow closely the orders of the central government. What's more, he also unified the written characters for the whole country so that everyone could understand each others' writings.

Qinshihuang was a very strict emperor who managed the country as if he was managing an army. He sent many laborers to construct the Great Wall of China. He built nationwide roads and a highway connecting the capital with the grasslands in the north. These transport facilities helped to defend the country against the ruthless enemy, the Xiongnu.

Indeed, there is one strange personal question about *Qinshihuang*. He had many sons, however, in history people never mentioned a word about his queen. Also, there was no folklore telling us anything about the first queen of China.

GAMES FOR FUN

Do you know the different persons who can best represent their respective period of time in Chinese history? Please put them at the right places on the time axis. Make sure you match the times correctly!

| Mao Zedong | Dr. Sun Yat-sen | Qinshihuang | Tangtaizong | Wen Jiabao |

221B.C   618   1912   1949   2008
Ancient China   Nowadays

Answers:

221B.C Qinshihuang
1912 Dr. Sun Yat-sen
2008 Wen Jiabao

618 Tangtaizong
1949 Mao Zedong

Shí   duō   yì   rénkǒu   shì

十多亿人口是

tóng   yī   gè   mínzú   ma

同一个民族吗？

Are More Than 1 Billion People of the Same Nationality?

Pre-reading Questions

1. How many nationalities does China have? Does she have more nationalities than the U.S.A.?

2. Ancient time people from the West had begun to live in China and gradually they became one of the ethnic groups of China. Do you know when did this start?

3. How many Chinese ethnic groups can you identify?

Zhōngguó   yǒu   duōshao   gè   mínzú

❶ 中国 有 多少 个 民族？

Zhōngguó   shì   yī   gè   duō   mínzú   guójiā   gòng   yǒu
中国 是 一 个 多 民族 国家，共 有 56

gè   mínzú   Qízhōng   Hànzú   rénkǒu   zuì   duō   zhàn   yǐshàng
个 民族。其中 汉族[1] 人口 最 多，占 90% 以上，

qítā   gè   mínzú   chēng   wéi   shǎoshùmínzú   Suǒyǒu   Zhōngguó
其他 55 个 民族，称 为 少数民族。所有 中国

de   mínzú   hé   qilai   chēng   wéi   Zhōnghuá   Mínzú
的 民族 合 起来，称 为 中华 民族。

Zhōngguó   yǒu   nàme   duō   mínzú   yīfāngmiàn   yīnwèi   Zhōngguó
中国 有 那么 多 民族，一方面 因为 中国

面积大，自古以来就有很多民族住在中国的土地上；另一方面，也因为中国历史长，不断[2]有新的民族加入。

人口最多的民族称为汉族，因为汉朝（公元前206年至公元220年）是中国一个强大[3]而且时间长的王朝。其实汉族不是一个单纯[4]的民族，汉朝的时候，很多人从中亚[5]来到中国住，北方一个强大的游牧[6]民族匈奴经常和汉朝打仗，后来战败了，南方的匈奴就搬到中国住，他们也变成汉族。北方的匈奴没有搬到中国，他们向西走，跟很多民族打过仗，几个世纪之后，到达欧洲，欧洲人称他们为"匈"。

后来，像匈奴那样加入到汉族的民族很多，今天我们已经分别不出谁是新加入的民族，谁是原来的汉族了。

GLOSSARY

1 汉族 the Han ethnic group   2 不断 continuous, constant
3 强大 powerful   4 单纯 simple, pure
5 中亚 Central Asia   6 游牧 nomad

Translation

❶ How many Nationalities is China composed of?

China is a multinational country with 56 nationalities. Among them, the Han nationality has the largest number of people, accounting for more than 90% of the total population. The remaining 55 nationalities are commonly known as ethnic minorities. All the nationalities come together to form the Chinese nation.

The reasons why China has so many nationalities are two-fold. On the one hand, China has had numerous races living in her vast territory since ancient times; on the other hand, the long history of China makes it possible for the unceasing inclusion of new nationalities.

Most people in China come from the Han nationality since the Han Dynasty (206 BC — 220 AD) was once strong with a relatively long history. Actually, the Han nationality is not a pure race. Many people came to China from Central Asia during the Han Dynasty. In the north, a strong nomadic tribe called the Xiongnu went to wars frequently with the Han Dynasty. After being defeated, the Southern Xiongnu settled in China and gradually became a part of the Han nationality. The Northern Xiongnu, instead of moving to China, went westwards to the battlefields with many other nationalities. After a few centuries, they extended into Europe and the Europeans called them "Hun".

Since then, like the Xiongnu, many nationalities have joined the Han nationality. Today, it is impossible for us to distinguish the joined nationalities from the original Han nationality.

❷ 中华 民族 是 怎样 形成 的？
Zhōnghuá Mmínzú shì zěnyàng xíngchéng de

Shísān yì rén de Zhōnghuá Mínzú shì jīngguò sān zhǒng

十三 亿 人 的 中华 民族，是 经过 三 种

qíngkuàng xíngchéng de

情况 形成 的。

Shǒuxiān běnlái zhù zài Zhōngguó de bùtóng mínzú

首先，本来 住 在 中国 的 不同 民族

yīnwèi jiéhūn huòzhě dǎzhàng jiànjiàn tǒngyī héchéng yī gè

因为 结婚[7] 或者 打仗[8]，渐渐 统一，合成 一 个

mínzú Zhège zuìchū xíngchéng de mínzú jiàozuò Huáxiàzú

民族。这个 最初 形成 的 民族，叫做 华夏[10]族。

Zhōnghuá Mínzú de huá zì jiùshì láizì Huáxiàzú

中华 民族 的 "华" 字，就是 来自 华夏族。

Qícì shì běifāng mínzú jìnrù Zhōngguó Zhōngguó

其次，是 北方 民族 进入 中国。中国

běifāng de gāoyuán tiānqì hěn lěng Zhù zài gāoyuán de

北方 的 高原，天气 很 冷。住 在 高原 的

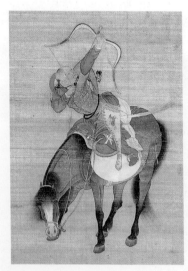

mínzú wèile dédào shíwù hé

民族，为了 得到 食物 和

yòngpǐn jīngcháng nán xià Zhèxiē

用品，经常 南 下[11]。这些

mínzú dōu hěn yǒnggǎn shànyú

民族 都 很 勇敢，善于[12]

dǎzhàng céngjīng zài Zhōngguó jiànlì

打仗，曾经 在 中国 建立

wángcháo Tāmen zuìchū shì zhàn

王朝。他们 最初 是 占

le běifāng bǎ Hànzú gǎn

了 北方，把 汉族 赶

dào nánfāng ér Měnggǔzú hé

到 南方；而 蒙古族 和

The Mongolian Tribe of the Yuan Dynasty

The founding emperor of the Yuan Dynasty — Genghis Khan

Mǎnzú dōu céngjīng wánquán
满族，都 曾经 完全
dǎbài Hànzú chéngwéi quán
打败 汉族，成为 全
Zhōngguó de zhǔrén Zhèxiē
中国 的 主人。这些
mínzú zhújiàn chéngwéi Zhōnghuá
民族 逐渐[13] 成为 中华
Mínzú de yī fènzǐ
民族 的 一 份子。

Dì sān zhǒng qíngkuàng
第 三 种 情况，
shì qítā mínzú yíjū dào
是 其他 民族 移居[14] 到
Zhōngguó Lìrú gōngyuán bā jiǔ shìjì shí cóng Zhōngyà hé
中国。例如 公元 八、九 世纪 时，从 中亚 和
Xīyà lái dào Zhōngguó de rén jiù yǒu chéngqiānshàngwàn Měnggǔ
西亚 来 到 中国 的 人，就 有 成千上万[15] 蒙古
tǒngzhì Zhōngguó shí cóng xīfāng
统治[16] 中国 时，从 西方
lái de rén gèng duō Hòulái
来 的 人 更 多。后来
bùshǎo xīfāngrén zìjǐ zǔchéng
不少 西方人 自己 组成
yī zú chēng wéi Huízú
一 族，称 为 回族。

The Muslim Tribal people

GLOSSARY

7	结婚	get married	8	打仗	fight, go to war
9	渐渐	gradually	10	华夏	archaic name for China
11	南下	go down south	12	善于	be good at
13	逐渐	gradually	14	移居	move one's residence, migrate
15	成千上万	thousands upon thousands	16	统治	rule, dominate

Translation

❷ How was the Chinese race formed?

The Chinese Nation with 1.3 billion people was shaped by three conditions.

First, due to war and marriage, different races united together gradually to form a nationality. This early nationality was called the Chinese Nation. The word "*Hua*" was derived from the term "*Huaxia*", for nationality.

Second, there were the invasions of the northern tribes into China. It was freezing cold to reside in the northern plateau. Such tribes usually went south to scramble for food and products. Being courageous fighters in war, they established empires in China. At the beginning, they dominated northern China and drove the Han nationality away to the south. Later, the Mongol and Manchu nationalities completely defeated the Han nationality, twice mastering all of China. These nationalities gradually became a part of the Chinese Nation.

The last was the migration of other nationalities into China. During the 8th — 9th centuries AD, hundreds and thousands of people moved to China from Central Asia and West Asia. Under the rule of Mongols, more and more people came from the west. Later, a number of westerners constituted an ethnic group called the Hui nationality.

❸ 中国 的 少数民族

中华 民族 里 有 五 个 人口 最多 的

民族，就是 汉族、满族、蒙古族、回族、藏族。

满族 和 蒙古族 曾经 建立 统治 全 中国

的 王朝。

13 世纪 时，蒙古族 建立 了 中国 第一

个 少数民族 王朝，叫做 元朝。回族 是

元朝 时 跟随 蒙古 人 从 西方 来 到 中国

居住 的。蒙古 族 强大 时，也 统治 西藏，

并且 相信 了 藏族 的 佛教，把 藏族 的 佛教

定 为 元朝 的 国教[17]，推广[18] 到 全 中国。

17 世纪 时，满族 和 蒙古族 一起 打败

汉族，第 二 次 建立 一 个 少数民族 王朝，

叫做 清朝。满族 也 统治 西藏，也 像 蒙古

人 那样，相信 了 藏族 的 佛教。满族 统治

了 中国 差不多 三 百 年。满族 学习 汉族 的

The Manchurian king and queen of the Qing Dynasty

wénhuà xué de hěn
文化， 学 得 很

hǎo yóuyú Mǎnzú
好， 由于 满族

rénshù shǎo yòu xué
人数 少， 又 学

le Hànzú de yǔyán
了 汉族 的 语言

hé xíguàn suǒyǐ
和 习惯¹⁹， 所以

hànhuà de hěn lìhai xiànzài yǐjing hěn shǎo rén jiǎng
汉化²⁰ 得 很 厉害， 现在 已经 很 少 人 讲

Mǎnyǔ le Bùguò xiànzài Zhōngguó hěn duō fēngsú céngjīng
满语²¹ 了。 不过， 现在 中国 很 多 风俗²²， 曾经

shòudào Mǎnzú yǐngxiǎng
受到 满族 影响。

GLOSSARY

17 国教 state religion
18 推广 populized
19 习惯 custom
20 汉化 Chinese localization
21 满语 the language of the Man ethnic group
22 风俗 custom

Translation

❸ The ethnic minorities of China

The top five nationalities with the highest populations were the Han nationality, Manchu nationality, Mongol nationality, Hui nationality and Tibetan nationality.

The Manchu and Mongol nationalities had once ruled China by establishing their own empires.

During the 13th century, the Mongol nationality founded the Yuan Dynasty, which was the first dynasty ruled by a national minority in China. The Hui nationality came along with the Mongols from the west to reside in China at that time. Tibet was once under the influence of the strong Mongol Empire. The Mongols even believed in Tibetan Buddhism and introduced it to China as a national religion.

When it came to the 17th century, the Han nationality suffered a second defeat under a joint effort by both the Manchu and Mongol nationalities. The national minorities founded another empire known as the Qing Dynasty. Similar to the Mongols' rule, the Manchu believed in Tibetan Buddhism after ruling over China. The Manchu rule lasted for almost 300 years. They had a good grasp of the Han culture. As the number of Manchu was small and they had learned the Han language and culture for some time, they became more and more like the Han nationality. Nowadays, not many people are able to speak the Manchu language. Nevertheless, many existing Chinese customs are proved to have been influenced by the Manchu.

The Chinese Republic of Five Ethnic Groups

The last ruling dynasty in China was the Qing Dynasty founded by the Manchu. Therefore, the last emperor of China was a Manchu. Afterwards, China experienced a revolutionary movement. The revolutionaries overthrew the Qing Dynasty and established the Republic. Dr. Sun Yat-sen, the leader of the revolution, immediately advocated the idea of "the Chinese Republic of Five Ethnic Groups". The five ethnic groups were the Han nationality, the Manchu nationality, the Mongol nationality, the Hui nationality and the Tibetan nationality. The Chinese Republic of Five Ethnic Groups was established to set up the republic equally for the five main ethnic groups, with there also being other smaller national minorities such as the Miao and Yao. The Manchu were not repelled. The Manchu Emperor did not leave the imperial palace. Actually he had lived in the imperial palace for 13 more years receiving a fixed living expense every year until the coming of a warlord who expelled him from the imperial palace in 1924.

GAMES FOR FUN

Please look at the pictures and can you identify the special characteristic of each of them? Please match the names of the ethnic groups with the respective pictures.

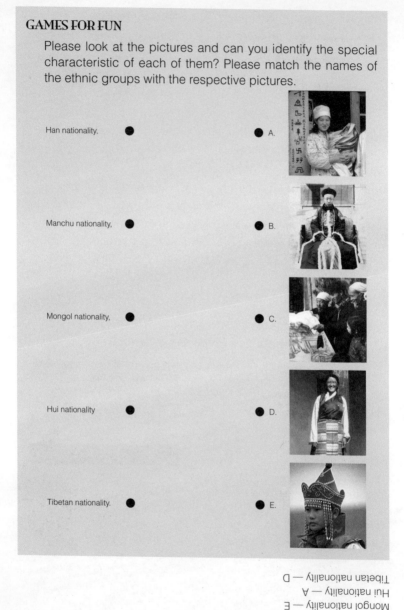

Han nationality, ●   ● A.

Manchu nationality, ●   ● B.

Mongol nationality, ●   ● C.

Hui nationality ●   ● D.

Tibetan nationality. ●   ● E.

Zhōngguórén xìn shénme zōngjiào

中国人信什么宗教？

What are the religions that Chinese people believe in?

Pre-reading Questions

1. Can Chinese worship the religion of Christianity as Protestants or as Catholics?

2. We frequently see the picture symbols of Taichi and the Eight Trigrams. Do you know which religion these two symbols originated from?

3. Until now what are the religions that still exist in China?

---

❶ Zhōngguó běntǔ zōngjiào
中国 本土 宗教

Zhōngguó shì yī gè duō zōngjiào
中国 是 一 个 多 宗教

de guójiā dànshì Zhōngguórén de
的 国家，但是 中国人 的

zōngjiào guānniàn bù nónghòu Zhōngguó yě
宗教 观念 不 浓厚[1]。中国 也

méiyǒu guīdìng de guójiào
没有 规定 的 国教。

The Taichi Symbol

Zhōngguó tǔshēngtǔzhǎng de zōngjiào jiàozuò Dàojiào shì
中国 土生土长[2] 的 宗教，叫做 道教[3]，是

yī zhǒng duōshénjiào Zhōngguó yǒu gè zhùmíng zhéxué jiā jiàozuò
一 种 多神教[4]。中国 有 个 著名 哲学家[5]，叫做

A Taoist temple of China

老子，他 认为 人 应该 明白 宇宙 的 道理，这
种 道理 叫做 "道"。道教 和 老子 本来 没有
关系，但是 把 老子 当作 祖师[6]。道教 最 特别
的，是 相信 人 可以 不 死，经过 学习 和 吃
药，成为 神仙[7]。神仙 不 一定 住 在 天上，
可以 住 在 仙山 里。

　　道教徒 用 金属 和 植物 做 实验，希望
做 出 不 死 药，有人 认为 他们 是 很 优秀
的 化学家。

由于 中国 的 宗教
Yóuyú Zhōngguó de zōngjiào

观念 不 浓厚，对 很
guānniàn bù nónghòu duì hěn

多 宗教 都 能够 包容[8]，
duō zōngjiào dōu nénggòu bāoróng

所以 很 少 发生 宗教
suǒyǐ hěn shǎo fāshēng zōngjiào

战争。佛教 传 到 中国
zhànzhēng Fójiào chuán dào Zhōngguó

之后，影响 很 大，和
zhīhòu yǐngxiǎng hěn dà hé

佛教 互相 吸收 对方 的
Fójiào hùxiāng xīshōu duìfāng de

思想。后来 中国人 还 把
sīxiǎng Hòulái Zhōngguórén hái bǎ

儒家 也 当作 宗教，称
Rújiā yě dàngzuò zōngjiào chēng

为 儒教[9]，把 道教、佛教、
wéi Rújiào bǎ Dàojiào Fójiào

The founder of the Taoist religion — Lao Zi

儒教 集合 在 一 个 寺庙 里 崇拜[10]，叫做 三 教
Rújiào jíhé zài yī gè sìmiào li chóngbài jiàozuò sān jiào

合 一。这 是 中国 宗教 的 特色[11]。
hé yī Zhè shì Zhōngguó zōngjiào de tèsè

GLOSSARY

1 浓厚 dense, strong, pronounced; pronounced or marked local color
2 道教 Taoism
3 土生土长 be indigenous to
4 多神教 polytheistic
5 哲学家 philosopher
6 祖师 founder
7 神仙 supernatural being
8 包容 contain; include
9 儒教 Confucianism
10 崇拜 worship; adore
11 特色 characteristic

Translation

❶ The Indigenous Religion of China

China is a multi-religious country. But the Chinese do not have a strong belief in religion. China does not have a commonly accepted national religion either. The indigenous religion of China is called Taoism, a religion worshipping many gods. There was a very famous philosopher in China called Lao Zi. He believed that people should understand the philosophical reasoning of the universe. He called this philosophy, Tao. Basically Lao Zi was not related to Taoism but he was regarded as the founder of Taoism, which had this idiosyncratic belief in immortality. The Taoists believed that through religious study and ingestion of medicine people could become immortal beings, who did not necessarily have to live in heaven. They could live in the mountain for the immortals.

Taoists experimented with metals and plants hoping to produce the medicine of immortality. Some people thought that they were excellent chemists. Since the Chinese did not have a strong belief in religion many religions were allowed to be practiced in China. There were hardly any wars due to religions. After the spread of Buddhism into China it exerted a great deal of influence on the Chinese. Buddhism and Taoism had absorbed each other's philosophy. Later on the Chinese also considered Confucianism as a form of religion and it was placed together with Taoism, and Buddhism in the same temple for worshipping. This practice was called a three-in-one religious confederation. In this respect the Chinese are unique in their religious expression.

❷ 中国 最早 的 外来 宗教

自 古 以 来[12]，西方 的 宗教 就 不断 传

入 中国。佛教 是 最 早 传 到 中国 的 西方

宗教。大约 在 公元 一 世纪，已经 由 印度

传 来。佛教 没有 神，创立 佛教 的 是 佛陀[13]，

佛陀 是 觉悟[14] 者 的 意思。最初 中国人 并 不

了解 佛教，把 佛陀 当作 很 多 神 里面 的

一 个。后来 很 多 佛教徒[15] 由 中亚、波斯[16]、

印度 来 中国，中国 的 佛教徒 也 到 新疆[17]

和 印度 学习 佛经[18]，中国人 才 明白 佛教 的

道理。佛教徒 要 出家[19]，而 中国 重视 孝，

所以 知识分子[20] 曾经 大力 反对 佛教。后来

佛教 吸收 了 中国 的 思想，很 快 就 成为

中国 重要 的 宗教。因为 中国人 很 喜欢

佛教，所以 深入 研究 它，提 出 自己 的 理解

和 学说。禅宗 就是 中国化 的 佛教 学说[21]。

A Buddhist temple in the area where the Han race reside
— the Jade Buddha temple of Shanghai

Zhīshifènzǐ　tèbié　xǐhuan　chánzōng　hái　fāzhǎn　chu　chán　shī
知识分子 特别 喜欢 禅宗，还 发展 出 禅 诗、

chán huà hé yǒu chánwèi de yuánlín hòulái chuán dào Rìběn
禅 画 和 有 禅味 的 园林²³，后来 传 到 日本。

Zhōngguó shì yī gè duō mínzú guójiā yǒuxiē zōngjiào
中国 是 一 个 多 民族 国家，有些 宗教

de chuánbō yǔ shǎoshùmínzú yǒu guānxi Lìrú Fójiào yǒu
的 传播 与 少数民族 有 关系。例如 佛教 有

yī pài jiàozuò Mìzōng fēnbié jīngguò Xīnjiāng hé Xīzàng
一 派 叫做 密宗，分别 经过 新疆 和 西藏

chuán lái Zhōngguó qízhōng chuán rù Xīzàng de mìzōng jīntiān
传 来 中国，其中 传 入 西藏 的 密宗，今天

chēng wéi Zàng chuán Fójiào Měnggǔ qiángdà de shíhou tǒngzhì
称 为 藏 传 佛教²⁴。蒙古 强大 的 时候，统治

A tibetan Buddhist temple in the northwest territories of China
— the La Bu Leng Temple

Xīzàng　hòulái　gǎi　xìn　le　Zàng　chuán　Fójiào　zài　Xīzàng

西藏，后来 改 信 了 藏 传 佛教，在 西藏

yǐwài　de　Zhōngguó　dìfang　jiàn　le　hěn　duō　Zàng　chuán　fósì

以外 的 中国 地方，建 了 很 多 藏 传 佛寺。

GLOSSARY

12 自古以来　from of old　　13 佛陀　Buddha
14 觉悟　awaken; enlighten　　15 佛教徒　Buddhist
16 波斯　Persia
17 新疆　Xinjiang, a province in the North China　　18 佛经　sutra
19 出家　become a monk or nun; enter into religion
20 知识分子　intellectual　　21 学说　theory; doctrine
22 禅宗　Zen　　23 园林　garden
24 藏传佛教　Buddhism from Tibet

Translation

❷ The Earliest Foreign Religion Imported into China

Since ancient times, Western religions have spread into China. Buddhism was the earliest one. Approximately in the first century A.D. it had come through India. Buddhism does not have a god. It was founded by Buddha, which literally means *awakened one or enlightened one*. In the beginning, the Chinese did not understand Buddhism and worshipped Buddha as one of the many gods they had been worshipping. Later on many Buddhists came to China from the Middle East, Persia and India to preach. Chinese Buddhists also went to Xinjiang and India to study the Scriptures of Buddhism. After all these activities the Chinese finally had a good understanding of the philosophy of Buddhism. Devoted Buddhists have to leave their family to become monks. This practice is contradictory to the highly regarded Confucius practice of filial piety. At one time the intellectuals of China were strongly against Buddhism. Later on Buddhism acclimatised itself into the philosophy of China and rapidly became a significant religion. Because the Chinese had a special liking of Buddhism it had been researched in depth and some Chinese scholars further philosophised Buddhism with their own interpretations, forming some schools of thoughts with those interpretations. Zen Buddhism is one of these "sinicized" Buddhist sects. The Chinese intellectuals specially favoured Zen Buddhism. They also developed the Zen way of poetry writing, painting and gardening. These techniques were later imported into Japan.

China is a multi-racial country. The spread of some religions has been related to some minorities. For instance one form of Buddhism, called *Mizong* (密宗) was imported into China from Xinjiang and Tibet. It has since then remained in Tibet and this is the reason why it has been contemporarily renamed as Tibetan Buddhism. During the historic period when the Mongols were strong they ruled Tibet and worshipped Tibetan Buddhism. They also built many Tibetan Buddhist temples outside of Tibet.

Hòulái chuán rù de Xīfāng zōngjiào
❸ 后来 传 入 的 西方 宗教

Yīsīlánjiào dà guīmó
伊斯兰教[25] 大 规 模

chuán rù Zhōngguó hé Měnggǔ
传 入 中国 和 蒙古

rén yǒu guānxi Yīsīlánjiào
人 有 关系。伊斯兰教

zài Tángcháo yǐjing chuán rù
在 唐朝 已经 传 入,

xìntú bù duō Měnggǔ xīzhēng
信徒[26] 不 多。蒙古 西征

zhīhòu hěn duō Zhōngyà hé
之后, 很 多 中亚 和

A Christian church in China — the Sophia Great Cathedral of Ha'erbin

Xīyà de Mùsīlín suí zhe Měnggǔ rén láidào Zhōngguó
西亚 的 穆斯林[27] 随 着 蒙古 人 来到 中国

dìngjū Mùqián Zhōngguó yuē yǒu wàn Mùsīlín
定居。目前,中国 约 有 1,800万 穆斯林。

Tiānzhǔjiào hé Jīdūjiào chuán dào Zhōngguó jiào wǎn
天主教 和 基督教[28] 传 到 中国 较 晚。

Jīdūjiào běnlái bāokuò Tiānzhǔjiào
基督教 本来 包括 天主教、

Xīnjiào Dōngzhèngjiào děng dànshì
新教[29]、东正教 等, 但是

zài Zhōngguó Jīdūjiào shì zhǐ
在 中国,基督教 是 指

Xīnjiào ér Luómǎ de Jīdūjiào
新教,而 罗马 的 基督教

jiàozuò Tiānzhǔjiào Zài Tángcháo
叫做 " 天主教 "。在 唐朝

chuán rù Zhōngguó dànshì fāzhǎn
传 入 中国,但是 发展

A Christian church in China, Guangzhou

不大。16 世纪 时，欧洲 传教士[30] 大量 东
来，天主教 再 传 到 中国。当时 的
传教士 借用 中国 的 词语 "天主" 来 称呼[31]
基督教 的 神。他们 调整 传教[32] 的 方法，
融合 中国 的 传统 观念，例如 拜 祖先 的
习惯，所以 得到 支持。可是 罗马 教会[33] 不
同意 他们 的 传教 方式。1840年 鸦片[34]战争，
中国 战 败，大量 天主教 和 基督教 的
传教士 来 中国 传教，与 中国人 发生 冲突[35]，
还 引起 战争。1950 年代 后，中国 大陆
的 天主教 脱离 罗马 教会。现在 中国 有
天主教徒 约 400 万 人。近年 基督教[36]在 中国
大陆 发展 很
快，现在 有
基督徒 约 一
千 万 人。

The mosque in China

25 伊斯兰教 Islam	26 信徒 believer
27 穆斯林 Muslim	28 基督教 Christianity
29 新教 Protestantism	30 传教士 missionary
31 称呼 appellation	32 传教 to do missionary work
33 教会 church	34 鸦片 opium
35 冲突 conflict	36 基督徒 Christian

Translation

❸ Other Religions that Spread to China

The large-scale importation of Islam into China was because of the Mongols. In the Tang Dynasty Islam had already come to China but there were not too many followers. After the Mongols furthered their invasion westward into the Middle East and Western Asia many Muslims followed the Mongols to China and they resided in China ever since. Today China has approximately 18,000,000 Muslims.

The Catholics and the Christians came to China quite a bit later. Basically Christianity includes Catholicism, Protestantism and the Orthodox Church. However in China when people mention Christianity they mean Protestantism. The Chinese call the Christian religion originating from Rome catholicism. It came to China during the Tang Dynasty but its propagation was limited. In the 16th century a large number of European missionaries came to Asia. They tried to rekindle the propagation of the Catholic religion. At that time those missionaries borrowed the Chinese terminology of *the heavenly god* to describe the Christian God. They adjusted their ways of preaching their religion and mixed their religious philosophy with the traditionally accepted social concepts of the Chinese. For example followers were allowed to keep their tradition of worshipping their ancestors. This was why they gained support among the people. Unfortunately the Roman Catholic Church disagreed with this modified practice of their faith and the Catholic religion went into decline again. In 1840 when the Chinese were defeated in the Opium War many Catholic and Protestant missionaries came to China to preach their religion, trying to recruit followers. Their activities caused conflicts with the local people and led to a war. After 1950 the Catholic religion in China broke away from the Roman Catholic Church. Today there are approximately 4 million Catholics in China. In recent years the number of Protestants has increased rapidly. There are about 10,000,000 Protestants in China.

Famous immortals

In China two of the most famous immortals are Xiwangmu and The Eight Immortals.
According to the recordings in the earliest novel of mythology in China *Shan Hai Jing* (*The Classic of Mountains and Seas*), Xiwangmu, a wicked character who possessed the medicine of everlasting life, lived in a cave in the West and in the same novel, *Shan Hai Jing*, this person's sex had not been identified and there was no mention of this character being a woman. Maybe because of the fact that the

A ceramic painting of the Eigth Immortals

Chinese character, Mu, meaning a mother was part of the name

The figure of Xiwangmu

of Xiwangmu people of later periods of time regarded this character as an old lady. Later on further developments of this character made her more and more beautiful and she finally emerged as a beautiful lady in her thirties and was always accompanies by a group of young girls. According to Chinese legends there were two Chinese Emperors who had met her and had become her good friends. They composed poems to give to one another.

Baxians are eight celestial beings in folklore. One of them was a lady. Another one was a young man and one of the eight immortals had a disabled leg! They all had their own special supernatural abilities. Therefore there is a saying in Chinese, "Eight immortals use their own special supernatural abilities to cross the sea in eight ingeniously different ways."

It means that different people can use different ways to solve the same hard to deal with problem. The stories of Xiwangmu and the Eight Immortals appear in many paintings and artcrafts of China.

GAMES FOR FUN

Can you identify which are the ones that can be described as the objects that symbolize religions? Please select them.

A. Buddhism B. Taoism C. Islam D. Christianism

(   )   (   )   (   )   (   )

(   )   (   )   (   )   (   )

Zhōngguó de jīng jì shì

中国的经济是

zěn yàng yī huí shì

怎样一回事？

How has the Chinese Economy Developed?

Pre-reading Questions

1. Today what are the influences of the Chinese economy on the world? Do they affect the U.S.A.?

2. Has the Chinese economy been affecting the world all the time?

Zhòngshì nóngyè

❶ 重视 农业

Zài Zhōngguó gǔdài guójiā de jīngjì yǒurú yī kē
在 中国 古代，国家 的 经济 有如 一 棵

dà shù nóngyè shì zhè kē shù de shù gēn Méiyǒu le
大 树，农业 是 这 棵 树 的 树 根[1]。没有 了

shù gēn shù jiù bù néng shēngcún Měi gè
树 根，树 就 不 能 生存[2]。每 个

cháodài de huángdì dōu hěn zhòngshì nóngyè
朝代 的 皇帝 都 很 重视[3] 农业。

Tāmen rènwéi zhǐyào nóngyè fāzhǎn de
他们 认为，只要 农业 发展 得

hǎo yǒu zúgòu de liángshi shèhuì jiù huì
好，有 足够 的 粮食，社会 就 会

āndìng
安定。

Farmers at work

为了 发展 农业，中国人 运河 和 水坝[4]，开垦[5] 了 大量 土地，种植 水稻[6]、小麦[7]、茶、棉花 等 农作物。两 千 多 年

A scene of a farmer at work in the Han Dynasty

前，中国人 就 已经 用 铁 做 农具[8] 了。

中国 的 手工业[9] 也 有 很 大 成就。中国 的 陶瓷[10]、丝绸 和 纸 促进[11] 了 世界 文明 的 进步[12]。15 世纪，中国 制造 的 船 曾经 航行 到 非洲。

发达 的 手工业 使 商业[13] 获得 发展。三千多年 前 的 王朝 叫做 商朝（公元 前 1600 年 — 公元 前 1046 年），商朝 人 很 善于 做 生意，所以 后来 做 生意 的 人 也 叫做 商人，做 生意 就 叫做 商业。商业 促进 了 城市 的 发展。长安（今 西安）、洛阳、北京 这些 城市 曾经 是 不同 王朝 的 首都，它们 都 非常

fánhuá 繁华[14]。而 近海 的 广州 和 泉州 成为 重要 的 港口[15]。世界 最早 的 纸币[16]也 出现 在 中国。

但是，在 经济 这 棵 大 树 上，商业 只是 它 的 树叶。为了 保证[17]农业 的 地位，皇帝 都 限制[18]商业，以免 商人 势力[19]太 大。

汉朝 政府 规定[20]：商人 不 能 坐 车，不 能 穿 丝绸 衣服，商人 和 他 的 孩子 都 不 能 做 官。

Since ancient times Guangzhou has been a trading port. Around this area there were many trading firms at one time.

GLOSSARY

1	树根	root		2	生存	survive
3	重视	pay attention to		4	水坝	dam
5	开垦	open up waste land		6	水稻	rice
7	小麦	wheat		8	农具	farm tools
9	手工业	handicraft industry		10	陶瓷	ceramics
11	促进	accelerate		12	进步	progress
13	商业	commerce		14	繁华	flourishing
15	港口	port		16	纸币	paper currency
17	保证	ensure		18	限制	restrict
19	势力	force		20	规定	stipulate

Translation

❶ The Importance of Agriculture

In ancient China, the state economy could be compared to a big tree of which agriculture was its roots. Without the roots, a big tree could not survive. All emperors laid much emphasis on agriculture. In their minds, as long as agriculture was well-developed, social stability would be ensured with a sufficient food supply.

To develop agriculture, the Chinese built dams and canals, and they also open up lands to plant crops such as rice, wheat, tea and cotton. Two thousand years ago, the Chinese had already used iron to make agricultural tools.

In addition, China was also known for its success in the handicraft industry. The invention of silk, paper and porcelain helped to foster the development of world civilization. In the 15th century, Chinese ships once made a voyage to the Africa.

The prosperity of the handicraft industry also made possible the development of trade. Three thousand years ago in the Shang Dynasty (1600 BC — 1046 BC), people were good at running businesses. So people doing business were later regarded as "traders" (商人, *Shangren*) whereas the business activities they were engaged in were known as "trade" (商业, *Shangye*). The commercial trade also brought the cities forward. Ancient cities like Chang'an (today's Xi'an), Luoyang and Beijing were once old capitals for many dynasties. They were flourishing at that time. The coastal cities of Guangzhou and Quanzhou became important ports. Even the earliest form of notes (paper currency) appeared in China.

However, trade was only the leaves on the big tree of the economy. To ensure the secure position of agriculture, the emperors tended to restrict trade to avoid the growing influence of traders. According to the laws of the Han Dynasty, merchants were not allowed to take carts or wear silk clothes. The merchant families could not have any positions in the government either.

❷ 1840 年后 的 中国 经济

中国 通过 丝绸 之 路[21]，跟 外国 做 生意。 不过 中国 的 农业 和 手工业 都 很 发达[22]，除了 奢侈品[23]，中国 只 会 买 少量 外国 的 东西。 欧洲 工业 革命[24] 之后，工业 发达，要 向 中国 卖 工业 品。1840 年 中国 战 败，被迫[25] 大量 与 欧洲 通商[26]，进行 不 平等 的 贸易[27]。外国 商品 的 关税[28] 很 低，后来，连 中国 海关[29] 也 被 外国 控制 了。外国 人 可以 自由 地 在 中国 开 工厂、采 矿[30]、修建 铁路。中国 传统 经济[31] 衰落[32] 了。

于是，一些 中国人 认为 办 企业[33] 能够

An ironworks toward the end of the Qing Dynasty

shǐ guójiā fùqiáng,[34] tāmen xuéxí xīfāng de jìshù, yǐnjìn[35]
使 国家 富强[34]，他们 学习 西方 的 技术，引进[35]

wàiguó de jīqì. Zài Tiānjīn Shànghǎi Guǎngzhōu děng yánhǎi
外国 的 机器。在 天津、上海、广州 等 沿海

chéngshì, chūxiàn le chuán chǎng jīqì chǎng sīchóu chǎng hé
城市，出现 了 船 厂、机器 厂、丝绸 厂 和

mòfáng, fǎngzhīyè, miànfěnyè[36] de chǎnliàng zēngjiā le hěn
磨坊，纺织业、面粉业[36] 的 产量 增加 了 很

duō. Zhōngguórén yě bàn hángyùnyè, cǎi kuàngchǎng hé yínháng.
多。中国人 也 办 航运业、采矿厂 和 银行。

Dànshì, hòulái Zhōngguó yòu jīnglì le Rìběn rùqīn hé
但是，后来 中国 又 经历 了 日本 入侵 和

nèizhàn. Suǒyǐ jǐnguǎn[38]
内战。所以 尽管[38]

Zhōngguórén fùchū jùdà
中国人 付出 巨大

de nǔlì, Zhōngguó de
的 努力，中国 的

jīngjì háishi shòudào
经济 还是 受到

chénzhòng[39] de dǎjī[40].
沉重[39] 的 打击[40]。

A tribal entrepreneur toward the end of the Qing Dynasty – Zhang Jian. He founded one of the industrial bases of modern China.

GLOSSARY

21	丝绸之路	the Silk Road	22	发达	developed
23	奢侈品	luxury goods	24	工业革命	the Industrial Revolution
25	被迫	be forced	26	通商	trade
27	贸易	trade	28	关税	customs duty
29	海关	customs	30	采矿	mining
31	传统经济	traditional economy	32	衰落	decline
33	企业	enterprise	34	富强	prosperous and strong
35	引进	import	36	面粉业	flour industry
37	航运业	shipping industry	38	尽管	although
39	沉重	heavy	40	打击	blow

Translation

❷ The Chinese Economy after the 1840's

China started its trade with other countries through the Silk Road. As agriculture and the handicraft industries prospered in China, China seldom bought exotic things except luxury items. After the Industrial Revolution, the European industries thrived and thus these countries intended to sell their industrial products to China. In 1840, China was defeated in war and was forced to trade extensively on unequal terms with the European countries. The tariffs were set rather low for exotic goods. Later, even the Chinese customs office was under the control of foreign countries. Foreigners were free to set up factories, do mining and construct railways. China's traditional economy collapsed.

Some Chinese considered strengthening the country by starting enterprises. They learned the western technology and introduced foreign machinery to China. Ship factories, machine factories, silk factories and mills were all founded in coastal cities like Tianjin, Shanghai and Guangzhou. The output of the textile and flour industries also increased greatly. In addition, the Chinese also set up the shipping industry, mining, factories and banks. Nevertheless, China experienced the invasion of Japan followed by a civil war. The Chinese economy suffered heavy blows despite the people's great efforts.

❸ 当代 中国 经济

Dāngdài Zhōngguó jīngjì

1949 年 中华 人民 共和国 成立 后，实行
nián Zhōnghuá Rénmín Gònghéguó chénglì hòu shíxíng

公有制[41] 经济 和 计划 经济。每 五 年 设立 一
gōngyǒuzhì jīngjì hé jìhuà jīngjì Měi wǔ nián shèlì yī

个 经济 发展 的 目标。那时，中国 大力 发展
gè jīngjì fāzhǎn de mùbiāo Nàshí Zhōngguó dàlì fāzhǎn

重工业[42] 和 国防 工业[43]；工业化 速度 很 快。
zhònggōngyè hé guófáng gōngyè gōngyèhuà sùdù hěn kuài

但是，农业 和 轻工业[44] 发展 比较 慢。由于
Dànshì nóngyè hé qīnggōngyè fāzhǎn bǐjiào màn Yóuyú

缺少 日常 生活 用品，当时 中国人 的 生活
quēshǎo rìcháng shēnghuó yòngpǐn dāngshí Zhōngguórén de shēnghuó

水平 不 高。1978 年，中国 实行"改革 开放"
shuǐpíng bù gāo nián Zhōngguó shíxíng gǎigé kāifàng

政策，经济 快速 发展 起来。中国 的 经济 总
zhèngcè jīngjì kuàisù fāzhǎn qǐlái Zhōngguó de jīngjì zǒng

量[45]上升 到 世界 前 几 位。人民 的 生活 水平
liàng shàngshēng dào shìjiè qián jǐ wèi Rénmín de shēnghuó shuǐpíng

The village and the farmland

也 大 有 提高。中国 市场 大，吸引 了 很 多
外国 企业 来 投资⁴⁶。他们 都 看 好 中国 经济
的 前景⁴⁷。

今天 中国 的 经济 结构⁴⁸中，农业 仍然
是 重要 的，60% 的 人口 是 农民。中国 农业
不仅 为 世界 四 分之 一 的 人口 提供 粮食，
还 有 大量 农产品 出口 到 国外，例如 2007
年 中国 蔬菜 的 出口 量⁴⁹就 列 全 世界 第一
位。水果、茶叶 等 农产品 的 产量⁵⁰都 是
世界 最 多 的。但是
加工业⁵¹ 对 中国 经济
发展 贡献⁵²也 很 大，中国
的 食品 加工、塑料⁵³
加工、玩具、家用 电器、
纺织业 等 在 全球 经济
中 占有 很 大 的 比重⁵⁴。

An area that produces tea — a tea plantation

41 公有制 public ownership   42 重工业 heavy industry
43 国防工业 national defense industry 44 轻工业 light industry
45 经济总量 total supply and demand   46 投资 invest
47 前景 prospect   48 结构 structure
49 出口量 export quantity   50 产量 output
51 加工业 processing industry   52 贡献 contribution
53 塑料 plastics   54 比重 proportion

Translation

❸ The Contemporary Chinese Economy

In 1949, with the establishment of the People's Republic of China, China implemented a socialist planned economy. It set up a goal for economic development once every five years. At that time, it developed heavy industries and defense industries with all its effort. The pace of industrialization ran fast. By comparison, agriculture and light industry just developed slowly. Due to a lack of daily necessities, the standard of living was not high. In 1978, China implemented the policy of "Opening the country through reforms" by which the economy flourished rapidly. China's economic output has already reached the top few in the world. The standard of living has been making great strides. As it offers a big market, China has attracted hundreds and thousands foreign enterprises to invest in the country. These enterprises have confidence in the prospects of the Chinese economy.

Today in China's economic structure, agriculture still constitutes an important part. Sixty percent of the population is the peasantry. The agriculture of China not only provides food for one-fourth of the world population, it also exports a wealth of crops to other countries. For instance, in 2007, China ranked first in exporting vegetables in the world. Other crops like fruit and tea also get the first place in their world output. Moreover, processing industries have also made great contributions to the Chinese economy. China's food processing, plastics processing, toys, home appliances, and textile industry all add up to a high proportion of the global economy.

The three great economic zones of China:

Now, China has three busy economic regions, namely, the Yangtze River Delta, the Pearl River Delta and the Bohai Bay Area.

The Yangtze River Delta

The Yangtze River Delta drains into the East China Sea. It is the estuary of the largest river, the Yangtze River, in China. Shanghai is at the center of this delta which is the busiest economic zone in China. It is easily accessible by public transportation. Urbanization is the most common phenomenon here with a high concentration of cities. A pool of talent with sound education backgrounds is found in this region to form the most comprehensive labor base in China.

The Pearl River Delta

The Pearl River Delta, situated at the estuary of the Pearl River, is facing the South China Sea. It is comprised of some Guangdong provincial cities such as Guangzhou and Shenzhen. Adjacent to Hong Kong and Macau, it is equipped with well-established foreign connections, and is easily accessible by land and sea transportation. This region was open to foreign trade a long time ago. The electronics industry, light industry and service industry all play a leading role in China.

The Bohai Bay Area

The Bohai Bay Area lies on the northern part of Eastern China along the coast with Bejing and Tianjin as its center. It includes Inner Mongolia and Liaoning province as well. This area provides an important link to the world for Northern China. Abundant in natural resources, it has become the source for coal and petroleum. Therefore, heavy industry was able to develop a long time ago, for instance, the machinery, chemical, automobile, and iron and steel industries.

GAMES FOR FUN

Look at the following pictures. They are all about various professions in China. You may also visit these websites: www.taobao.com, www.eachnet.com, www.amazon.cn to see how the Chinese go online shopping. If you were going to run a business in China, which kind of business would you like to try? Why?

The sinicized fast food restaurants, which are conceived and run by Chinese, are quite popular in China.

When Chinese people spend time wandering around the streets to window shop they like to have small snacks accompanied by soft drinks. This is why snack-food shops are doing very good business.

MacDonald's in China

In many Chinese cities there are a lot of these privately owned and operated "motored taxis" in operation.

Chinese people like to buy computers at computer markets.

In China there are a lot of small shops like these, selling handicrafts and quality goods. They attract a lot of travelling traders from all over the world.

Wèi shénme Zhōngguórén de

为什么中国人的

kǎoshì chéngjì hǎo

考试成绩好？

Why are the Examination Results of the Chinese Students Consistently Good?

Pre-reading Questions

1. What are the examinations that Chinese students in China have to pass before they can enter universities for further education?
2. The Chinese people always put a heavy emphasis on examinations. Do you know the reason?

Zhōngguó zhòngshì jiàoyù de chuántǒng

❶ 中国 重视 教育 的 传统

Hěn duō rén dōu juéde qíguài wèishénme Zhōngguórén

很 多 人 都 觉得 奇怪，为什么 中国人

zài xuéxí shang biǎoxiàn chūsè Zhōngguórén xuéxí hǎo

在 学习 上 表现 出色[1]? 中国人 学习 好，

shì yīnwèi Zhōngguó zìgǔ yǒu zhòngshì jiàoyù de chuántǒng

是 因为 中国 自古 有 重视 教育 的 传统。

Sānqiānduōnián qián Zhōngguó jiù yǒu xuéxiào Dàn zhǐyǒu guìzú

三千多年 前 中国 就 有 学校。但 只有 贵族[2]

cáinéng jìnrù xuéxiào xuéxí Dànshì Kǒngzǐ gōngyuán qián

才能 进入 学校 学习。但是，孔子（公元 前

nián zhì qián nián dǎpò le zhè zhǒng zuòfǎ Tā

551 年 至 前 479 年）打破 了 这 种 做法。他

60

tíchū   yǒujiàowúlèi   de
提出 " 有教无类 " 的

sīxiǎng   yìsi   shì   jiàoyù
思想，意思 是 教育

yīng   bù   fēn   guójiā   yǔ
应 不 分 国家 与

mínzú   bù   fēn   guìzú
民族，不 分 贵族

yǔ   píngmín   suǒyǒu   de   rén
与 平民³，所有 的 人

dōu   kěyǐ   jiēshòu   jiàoyù
都 可以 接受 教育。

Kǒngzǐ   zìjǐ   jiù   shōu
孔子 自己 就 收

le   sān   qiān   míng   xuésheng
了 三 千 名 学生。

The famous educator in ancient China — Confucius

Zhège   sīxiǎng   tíchū   hòu   chǎnshēng   le   hěn   dà   de   yǐngxiǎng
这个 思想 提出 后，产生⁴ 了 很 大 的 影响。

Zhōngguórén   fēicháng   zūnjìng   Kǒngzǐ   duì   tā   de   huà   yě   hěn
中国人 非常 尊敬⁵ 孔子，对 他 的 话 也 很

xìnfú   Suǒyǐ   yǒujiàowúlèi   yìzhí   shì   Zhōngguó   jiàoyù   de
信服⁶。所以 " 有教无类 " 一直 是 中国 教育 的

yuánzé   Zhídào   jīntiān   Zhōngguórén   réngrán   zūnjìng   Kǒngzǐ
原则⁷。直到⁸ 今天，中国人 仍然 尊敬 孔子，

fēicháng   zhòngshì   jiàoyù
非常 重视 教育。

GLOSSARY

1 出色	outstanding	2 贵族	noble
3 平民	the common people	4 产生	bring out
5 尊敬	respect	6 信服	be convinced
7 原则	principle	8 直到	until

Translation

❶ China puts a heavy emphasis on education as a tradition

Many people find it strange and wonder why do Chinese people always perform outstandingly well in studying? The reason why Chinese people do well in studying is because of a tradition which has been established since ancient China. This tradition puts a very heavy emphasis on education. Schools existed in China over 3,000 years ago, but they were only for the aristocrats who were the privileged ones receiving their education in places resembling modern schools. Confucius (551 BC — 479 BC) revolutionized this discriminatory arrangement. He advocated his social philosophy of "*you jiao wu lei*" (有教无类) , meaning that education should be available to all students, irrespective of their countries of origin and their races. Students should not be classified into the two exclusive categories of the aristocrats and the common people. All should have the same opportunity to receive the same kind of education. He himself set an example and had over 3,000 students. The popularization of this social philosophy had a huge influence. The Chinese people respected Confucius very much then and they believed in his teaching. Up to this day, Chinese people still believe in Confucius and still highly regard education as one of the most important aspects of life.

❷ 中国 古代 的 学校
Zhōngguó gǔdài de xuéxiào

古代 不光[9] 政府
Gǔdài bùguāng zhèngfǔ

办 学校，私人 也[9] 办
bàn xuéxiào sīrén yě bàn

学校，而且 有些 私人
xuéxiào érqiě yǒuxiē sīrén

学校 水平 很 高，有
xuéxiào shuǐpíng hěn gāo yǒu

很 多 学生 努力 争取[10]
hěn duō xuésheng nǔlì zhēngqǔ

进去 读书。有 一 个
jìnqu dúshū Yǒu yī gè

A famous college in HuNan China — the Yue Lu College

学生 为了 请 一 名 姓 程 的 老师 收 他 做
xuésheng wèile qǐng yī míng xìng Chéng de lǎoshī shōu tā zuò

学生，在 老师 门 外 雪地 上 等 了 大 半 天。
xuésheng zài lǎoshī mén wài xuědì shang děng le dà bàn tiān

这个 故事 后来 成为 一 个 成语[11] ——"程 门
Zhège gùshi hòulái chéngwéi yī gè chéngyǔ chéng mén

立 雪"。
lì xuě

私人 办 的 学校 有 两 种 程度：基础
Sīrén bàn de xuéxiào yǒu liǎng zhǒng chéngdù jīchǔ

程度 的 学校，和 高等[12] 程度 的 书院[13]。基础
chéngdù de xuéxiào hé gāoděng chéngdù de shūyuàn Jīchǔ

程度 的 学校 主要 是 教 学生 认识 文字 和
chéngdù de xuéxiào zhǔyào shì jiāo xuésheng rènshi wénzì hé

写 文章。二 十 世纪 初，这些 学校 很 多
xiě wénzhāng Èr shí shìjì chū zhèxiē xuéxiào hěn duō

变成 了 现代 的 小学。而 书院 大约 从 公元
biànchéng le xiàndài de xiǎoxué Ér shūyuàn dàyuē cóng gōngyuán

shí shìjì kāishǐ jiù biànchéng jiàoxué hé yánjiū xuéwen de
十 世纪 开始，就 变成 教学[14] 和 研究 学问[15] 的

dìfang Shūyuàn de xiàozhǎng hěn zhòngyào Tāmen dōu shì hěn
地方。书院 的 校长[16] 很 重要。他们 都 是 很

yǒu míngwàng de xuéwen jiā jiàoxué hěn yángé xuésheng de
有 名望[17] 的 学问 家，教学 很 严格，学生 的

xuéyè yě jiào hǎo Shūyuàn dàduō yǐ xuésheng zìxué wéizhǔ
学业 也 较 好。书院 大多 以 学生 自学 为主，

lǎoshī kěyǐ zìyóu jiǎngkè Lǎoshī hé xuésheng jīngcháng
老师 可以 自由 讲课。老师 和 学生 经常

yīqǐ zìyóu biànlùn bāokuò xuéshù zhèngzhì děng wèntí
一起 自由 辩论[18]，包括 学术[19]、政治 等 问题。

Yīqiānduōnián lái shūyuàn chéngwéi Zhōngguó zhòngyào de gāoděng
一千多 年 来，书院 成为 中国 重要 的 高等

jiàoyù jīgòu Xuésheng men
教育[20] 机构。学生 们

zài shūyuàn li tǎolùn zhèngzhì
在 书院 里 讨论 政治，

yǒushí huì biànchéng xuésheng yùndòng
有时 会 变成 学生 运动[21]。

Dào èr shí shìjì chū jiù
到 二 十 世纪 初，就

bùzài yǒu shūyuàn le
不再 有 书院 了。

The private schools of the Qing Dynasty

GLOSSARY

9 不光……也…… not only ... but also ...		10 争取 fight for	
11 成语 idiom		12 高等 higher level	
13 书院 academy		14 教学 teach	
15 学问 knowledge		16 校长 headmaster	
17 名望 famous		18 辩论 argue	
19 学术 academic		20 高等教育 higher education	
21 学生运动 student movement			

Translation

❷ The Schools of Ancient China

In ancient China, schools were not only run by the government, but they were also run by private individuals. Moreover, some of these privately run schools had a very high standard. There were a lot of students who tried very hard to get into them for a better education. There was a student who tried to enroll as a student into the study program of Teacher Cheng, a very good teacher. He stood in front of the teacher's door in the snow and waited for over half a day. Later on this story has become a proverb, "*cheng men li xue*" (程门立雪) , literally meaning the door of Cheng standing snow.

There were two kinds of standards among privately run schools, the fundamental standard (schools) and the advanced standard (colleges). Schools of the fundamental standard mainly taught students how to recognize and use characters and how to write literary articles. In the beginning of the twentieth century a lot of these schools became the primary schools of modern times. Approximately since the beginning of the tenth century AD, colleges had become teaching institutes as well as the organizations where knowledge was further refined and researched. The headmasters of colleges were very crucial for the colleges. They were usually very famous scholars. They were very strict in their way of teaching and as a result their students performed better in their studies. Within the college, students mainly conducted their own self-directed study programs. Teachers could lecture without restrictions on the topics of their choice. Teachers and students frequently engaged in free debates. The topics of discussion included scholarly problems as well as political issues. With a history of over one thousand years, colleges became very important institutes of higher education in China. In the colleges, the students' discussions of controversial political issues sometimes evolved into student social movements. In the beginning of the twentieth century, this kind of college faded away altogether.

❸ 科举制和今天的教育制度

读了书，人们就想加入政府，实现自己的政治理想[22]。中国自从七世纪就开始用科举制[23]选拔[24]官员。不分贵族与平民，人人都可以公平[25]竞争[26]。科举制到1905年停止，经历[27]1300多年，对中国产生了很大的影响。第一，科举制令普通人可以通过考试当上官员[28]，为政府发现了不少人才。从此不再只有贵族才能当官。今天，中国选拔官员也有公务员[29]考试。第二，科举制也使人更重视教育。很多人刻苦[30]读书，希望能做官。不过科举制也有不好的地方，很多学生读书只为应付[31]考试，不注重[32]实际应用。

The examination hall of the ancient Imperial Examination of China

66

Zhídào jīntiān, bùshǎo Zhōngguó xuésheng hái yǒu zhège quēdiǎn[33]。
直到 今天 , 不少 中国 学生 还 有 这个 缺点[33]。

Kējǔ zhì shì Zhōngguó xiàn gěi shìjiè de yī fèn lǐwù
科举 制 是 中国 献 给 世界 的 一 份 礼物。

Yīnwèi kējǔ zhì shì lìshǐ shang bǐjiào zǎo érqiě bǐjiào
因为 科举 制 是 历史 上 比较 早 而且 比较

wánshàn de kǎoshì zhìdù Xǔduō guójiā de kǎoshì zhìdù
完善[34] 的 考试 制度[35]。许多 国家 的 考试 制度

dōu shì xiàng Zhōngguó xuéxí de Yǒu rén shuō Yīngguó de
都 是 向 中国 学习 的。有 人 说 英国 的

wénguān kǎoshì biàn jièjiàn le kējǔ kǎoshì de fāngfǎ
文官 考试 便 借鉴[36]了 科举 考试 的 方法。

Zhōngguó de gǔdài jiàoyù yǒu wánbèi de jiàoxué
中国 的 古代 教育,有 完备[37] 的 教学

lǐlùn duì jīntiān de jiàoyù réngrán hěn yǒu bāngzhù
理论 , 对 今天 的 教育 仍然 很 有 帮助。

Bùguò jīntiān de Zhōngguó jiàoyù zhìdù shì xiàng Xīfāng
不过 , 今天 的 中国 教育 制度 是 向 西方

xuéxí de wúlùn Zhōngguó dàlù Táiwān huò Xiānggǎng dōu
学习 的。无论 中国 大陆、台湾 或 香港 , 都

cǎiqǔ jiǔ nián yìwù jiàoyù jí cóng xiǎoxué dào chūzhōng dōu
采取[38]九 年 义务[39]教育,即 从 小学 到 初中 都

miǎn jiāo xuéfèi
免 交 学费。

GLOSSARY

22	理想	ideal	23	科举制	imperial examination system
24	选拔	select	25	公平	fair
26	竞争	competition	27	经历	go through
28	官员	official	29	公务员	civil servant
30	刻苦	hardworking	31	应付	handle
32	注重	pay attention to	33	缺点	disadvantage
34	完善	perfect	35	制度	system
36	借鉴	draw lessons from	37	完备	complete
38	采取	adopt	39	义务	obligation

Translation

❸ The Imperial Examination System and the Educational System of Today

After acquiring enough knowledge people then had the desire to join the government in order to put their political ideals into practical reality. Since the seventh century, China had begun using the Imperial Examination System to select government officials. Candidates from aristocrats to common people could compete in this fair selection process on an equal basis. After operating for over 1,300 years, the Imperial Examination System ended in 1905. Nevertheless, it had created huge social influences in China. The first social influence was that this Imperial Examination System opened up a channel for ordinary people to become government officials, a privilege monopolized by the aristocrats before. As a result, the government discovered a lot of talented people. Today in China there is also an open examination through which anyone can become a government officer if qualified. The second social influence was that the Imperial Examination System had made people place even more emphasis on education. Many people studied very hard hoping to become a government official. But the Imperial Examination System also had its drawbacks. Students studied only for passing examinations. They did not pay enough attention to the practical applications of the knowledge they were learning. Up until today there are still quite a few Chinese students committing the same mistake of neglecting how to apply what they have learned. The Imperial Examination System is a gift offered by China to the world. The Imperial Examination System was a comparatively more effective and reliable examination system, and historically China adopted it comparatively earlier than other countries. Therefore many other countries have learned from the Chinese experience in running their Examination System. Some people have said that the British Government Examination for selecting Administrative and Executive Officers is a concept borrowed from the Chinese Imperial Examination System.

The ancient educational system in China had a very comprehensive set of theories of teaching and learning. Up until today it still helps education in China a lot. But the modern Chinese educational system is a system which has largely been adopted from the West. No matter it is in

China, in Taiwan or in Hong Kong the system of nine years of compulsory free education is being enforced. In other words students do not have to pay any school fees for nine years from primary school to junior middle school.

High School Education in China Today

The high school educational system in China today is very similar to that in Western countries.

After graduating from primary school, students then enter the program of junior middle school (abbreviated as "初中") to receive their further education in the three-year program of junior middle school. According to the regulations of the Chinese government, every citizen has the obligation to get his or her education in this three-year junior middle school program, which is considered to be the basic educational program. The major subjects include: Language training, Mathematics, English, Physics, Chemistry, Geography, Biology, Politics, Music, Art and Physical Education.

After graduating from junior middle School, students have three choices. The first choice is to enter the program of advanced level high school (abbreviated as "高中"). Or they can either choose to enter the program of professional schools or the program of occupational schools. Both of the latter two programs generally have a three-year educational schedule. They train professional and skilled specialists such as machinery manufacturing specialists, automobile repairs and maintenance specialists. The program of advanced level high school is also a three-year schedule program. The first year is a continuation of the basic program of the junior middle school. The second and third years are preparation to enter the higher educational programs in universities. In other words, students in this program are preparing to take their advanced level examination, called gao kao (高考) in Chinese. The advanced level examination is a special examination in China. Every student has to take this examination before he or she can get into the university of his or her choice. Every university has its own required score from the advanced level examination for recruiting students. If the student has good results in the advanced level examination he or she can get into a good university. In China, all well-known good universities are state-run public universities. The school fees of Chinese universities range from a few thousand to ten thousand or more of RMB (人民币). The school fees of good public universities are usually among the cheapest.

GAMES FOR FUN

This is a lessons schedule from the first year of the three-year advanced level high school program in China. If you were a student in this class:

1. How many hours of Language training lessons per week do you have to take?

2. How many different subjects per week do you have to learn?

3. What is the subject of the lesson scheduled as the third lesson on Wednesday morning?

4. From this timetable can you see any differences in lessons between Chinese advanced level high schools and American senior high schools? If you were the headmaster would you change this lesson schedule?

Class schedule:

	Monday	Tuesday	Wednesday	Thursday	Friday
Morning	Languages	Chemistry	English	Political Knowledge	Mathematics
	English	Physics	Mathematics	Chemistry	Biology
	Geography	Mathematics	Biology	English	Physics
	Mathematics	History	Physics	History	Languages
	Physical Education	English	Computer	Music	
	Noon Break 12:00 PM 14:45 PM				
Afternoon	Political Knowledge	Languages	Chemistry	Physical Education	English
	Class-meeting	Self-study	Languages	Maths	Geography
	Self-study	Training in Physical Education	Interest Groups	Art	Self-study
	End of the Daily Session 5:10 PM				

Note: It's about 40 minutes for each class in the middle schools in China.

Zhōngguó shì gè shànyú
中国是个善于
fāmíng de guójiā ma
发明的国家吗?

Is China a Country Which is Good at Invention?

Pre-reading Questions

1. Besides the Four Great Inventions, do you know any of the other ancient Chinese inventions that have had worldwide influence?

2. Why is the modern development of technology in China comparatively inferior to that of the U. S. A.?

Sì dà fāmíng
❶ 四 大 发明 (1)

Xǔduō wàiguó rén rènwéi Zhōngguó shì gè shànyú fāmíng
许多 外国 人 认为 中国 是 个 善于 发明

de guójiā kěshì hěn duō Zhōngguó rén bìng bù zhèyàng xiǎng
的 国家, 可是 很 多 中国 人 并 不 这样 想。

Wàiguó rén zhèyàng xiǎng yīnwèi Zhōngguó gǔdài yǒu hěn duō
外国 人 这样 想, 因为 中国 古代 有 很 多

fāmíng yǐngxiǎng hěn dà Zhōngguó rén bù shì zhèyàng xiǎng
发明, 影响 很 大; 中国 人 不 是 这样 想,

yīnwèi jìn jǐ bǎi nián Zhōngguó de kēxué shuǐpíng luòhòu
因为 近 几 百 年, 中国 的 科学 水平 落后[1]。

Shuō dào Zhōngguó de kēxué fāmíng dàjiā dōu zhīdao
说 到 中国 的 科学 发明, 大家 都 知道

的 是 四 大 发明：造 纸、印刷、火药、司南

（后来 变成 指南针）。现在 有些 中国人 认为

中国 不只 有 这 四 种 发明。这 四 种 发明

特别 受 其他 国家 的 人 推崇[2]，是 因为 它们

对 世界 影响 很 大，对 世界 文明 很 重要。

对 中国人 来 说，这 四 种 发明 也 是

很 实用[3] 的。就 用 造 纸 来 说，中国 没有

埃及 的 纸草[4]，也 没有 养 很 多 羊，不 能 将

字 写 在 羊皮 书 上。没有 纸 之前，中国人

要 把 字 刻 在 一 片 一 片 竹子 上，很 重，

很 不 方便。还 有 一 种 方法，是 写 在 丝绸

上，你 想 这 有 多 贵？所以 有 人 发明 用

树皮[5]、破 布、破 鱼网[6] 来 造 纸 的 方法，又

便宜，又 方便。

GLOSSARY

1	落后	fall behind	2	推崇	hold in esteem
3	实用	practical	4	纸草	the special kind of grass called cyperus rotundus
5	树皮	bark of trees	6	鱼网	fishnet

Translation

❶ The Four Great Inventions of China (1)

Many foreigners think that China as a country is good at invention but many Chinese people do not think so. The opinions of foreigners are based on the great influence on the world that many of the inventions invented by the ancient Chinese people had. Those Chinese people who disagree with them do so based on the fact that within the most recent few hundred years the level of science in China has been relatively backward.

Speaking of the scientific inventions of China, we all know the Four Great Inventions which are paper, printing, gunpowder and "Sinan". (司南, The south directional steering device which later on became the compass) Now, some Chinese people think that the ancient Chinese had quite a few more inventions besides the Four Great Inventions, which have received so much praise from the people of other countries for the special reason that these Four Great Inventions have had such an important influence on the world, and have been very important to world civilization.

To the Chinese people these four inventions have been very practical in their applications. As an example, the invention of paper was very significant to the Chinese because, unlike the Egyptians, China did not have the special kind of grass called cyperus rotundus. (It could be used to make papyrus for writing and painting) China did not have a lot of sheep either and therefore could not use pieces of sheepskin to write on. Before the invention of paper, the Chinese people had to carve their writings on pieces of bamboo cuttings, which were very heavy and very inconvenient. There was an alternative method, which was to use of pieces of silk for writing. Can you imagine how expensive this was? Therefore, someone invented the method of using the bark of trees, broken pieces of cloth, and broken fishnets to make paper which was cheap and convenient.

❷ 四大发明 (2)

Sì dà fāmíng

我们现在对四大发明知道得更多。

大家都说，造纸是公元105年蔡伦发明的，发现了公元前画在纸上的地图之后，我们知道蔡伦只是改良造纸的方法。活字印刷术是公元1041年毕升发明的。在活字印刷术之前，用雕刻[7]的木板来印刷，现在找到的最早的雕版印刷品，是公元868年的佛经。这两种印刷术都没有发明之前，就用手抄。可是从公元七世纪开始，中国的教育十分发达，要抄很多书，佛教也发达，要抄很多佛经。于是两种印刷术就出现了。

火药是想做神仙的宗教人士在

A fire cannon which is made by gunpowder.

The compass of ancient China —
a south-directional device

shíyànshì li nòng chulai de
实验室[8] 里 弄 出来 的。

Tāmen zuò le sānsì bǎi nián shíyàn
他们 做 了 三四 百 年 实验，

jiéguǒ méiyǒu chéngwéi shénxiān
结果 没有 成为 神仙，

què zài jiǔ shìjì zuò chu huǒyào
却 在 九 世纪 做 出 火药。

Zhōngguórén yòng xiānjìn de huǒyào
中国人 用 先进 的 火药

wǔqì dǐkàng Měnggǔ méiyǒu chénggōng
武器 抵抗[9] 蒙古，没有 成功，

Měnggǔ rén yòng huǒyào wǔqì xī zhēng yúshì huǒyào chuán dào
蒙古人 用 火药 武器 西征[10]，于是 火药 传到

Ālābó hé Ōuzhōu
阿拉伯 和 欧洲。

Sīnán shì liǎngqiānduōnián qián fāmíng de jīngguò jìn
司南 是 两千多年 前 发明 的，经过 近

yī qiān nián de gǎiliáng hòulái yòng zài hánghǎi de luópán
一 千 年 的 改良，后来 用 在 航海[11]的 罗盘

shang Mànmàn biànchéng le jīntiān de zhǐnánzhēn
上。慢慢 变成 了 今天 的 指南针。

GLOSSARY

7 雕刻 carve
9 抵抗 resist
11 航海 navigation of the seas

8 实验室 laboratory
10 西征 conquest of the West

Translation

❷ The Four Great Inventions of China (2)

We have now learned more about these Four Great Inventions.

It was said that Cai Lun invented the method of making paper in 105 AD. Then maps drawn on paper before the time of Christ were discovered. After this discovery it is now known that Cai Lun only added improvements to the method of making paper. The technology of movable-type printing was invented by Bi Sheng in 1041 A.D. Before the invention of movable-type printing, printing was done by using wooden boards carved with the material to be printed. Today the earliest piece of printed matter discovered is a piece of Buddhist sutra printed using a carved wooden board in 868 A.D. Before the invention of these two methods of printing, similar functions were carried out by hand copying. But this inefficient copying method could not meet the demand for material duplication in a rapid manner. Since the beginning of the seventh century in China, education as a form of social activity had been very actively promoted and developed. A lot of books had to be copied (for teaching and studying). Buddhism was also being actively and widely preached. (To supplement oral preaching), a lot of Buddhist Scriptures had to be copied (for distribution). Therefore the aforementioned two kinds of printing appeared.

Gunpowder was an accidental bioproduct produced in the experimental laboratories of religious people who wanted to become immortals. They did numerous experiments in a period of three to four hundred years. The result was that none of them succeeded in becoming an immortal. Nevertheless gunpowder was invented in some of those experiments in the ninth century. The Chinese used advanced forms of weapons loaded with gunpowder to defend themselves against the Mongols. They did not succeed. However, the Mongols used gunpowder-powered weapons in their conquest of the West (Eurasia and Eastern Europe now). Then the knowledge of using gunpowder spread to Arabia and Europe.

The south directional steering device was invented over 2,000 years ago. After being improved upon for close to 1,000 years it was used as a compass for navigation of the seas. Gradually it has become the compass of today (which is used for the purpose of getting the right direction whenever or wherever it is needed).

❸ 四大 发明 之 外
Sì dà fāmíng zhī wài

除了 四大 发明，中国 还有 很多 有趣
Chúle sì dà fāmíng Zhōngguó hái yǒu hěn duō yǒuqù

的 科学 技术。像 两千多年 前 开始 使用 的
de kēxué jìshù Xiàng liǎngqiānduōnián qián kāishǐ shǐyòng de

针灸[12] 和 脉 诊[13] 法。中国 的 药方 是 混合[14]
zhēnjiǔ hé mài zhěn fǎ Zhōngguó de yàofāng shì hùnhé

多种 草药 的，叫做 复方，世界 上 很多
duō zhǒng cǎoyào de jiàozuò fùfāng shìjiè shang hěn duō

地方 只用 单方。中国 的 文字 不 方便 计算，
dìfang zhǐyòng dānfāng Zhōngguó de wénzì bù fāngbiàn jìsuàn

但是 中国 的 数学家 还是 有 很高 的 成就。
dànshì Zhōngguó de shùxuéjiā háishi yǒu hěn gāo de chéngjiù

公元 前 一 世纪，中国 的 数学 书 就 提出
Gōngyuán qián yī shìjì Zhōngguó de shùxué shū jiù tíchū

毕氏 定理 的 例子；公元 五
Bì shì dìnglǐ de lìzi gōngyuán wǔ

世纪，中国 科学家 已经 将
shìjì Zhōngguó kēxuéjiā yǐjing jiāng

圆周率[15] 的 数 值[16] 计算 到 小数点
yuánzhōulǜ de shù zhí jìsuàn dào xiǎoshùdiǎn

后 第 7 位。在 天文学、预测[17]
hòu dì wèi Zài tiānwénxué yùcè

地震[18] 的 仪器[19]、工程 技术 方面，
dìzhèn de yíqì gōngchéng jìshù fāngmiàn

中国 也 有 很大 成就。例如
Zhōngguó yě yǒu hěn dà chéngjiù Lìrú

公元 132 年 制造 的 地动仪，
gōngyuán nián zhìzào de dìdòngyí

是 世界 上 最早 测定[20] 地震
shì shìjiè shang zuì zǎo cèdìng dìzhèn

A model for acupuncture-moxibustion

77

The first gadget that could predict the directions and the locations of earthquakes — a seismographic monitor

fāngwèi de yíqì Gōngyuán qián nián jiànzào de
方位 的 仪器。公元 前 256 年 建造 的

dūjiāngyàn shuǐlì gōngchéng zhídào jīntiān hái zài fāhuī
"都江堰"水利 工程[21],直到 今天 还 在 发挥[22]

jùdà de zuòyòng
巨大 的 作用。

GLOSSARY

12 针灸 acupuncture and moxibustion
13 脉诊 diagnosis by feeling the pulse medical application
14 混合 mix
15 圆周率 ratio of the circumference of a circle to its diameter
16 数值 digit   17 预测 forecast
18 地震 earthquake   19 仪器 instrument
20 测定 estimate   21 水利工程 irrigation projects
22 发挥 make contribution

Translation

❸ Other Significant Chinese Inventions Besides the Four Great Inventions

Besides the Four Great Inventions, the Chinese people still have many interesting scientific technological accomplishments, such as acupuncture and moxibustion, diagnosis by feeling the pulse (medical application) which started to be used over 2,000 years ago. In China the prescriptions used in traditional Chinese medicine were mixtures of many different kinds of herbs, called compound prescriptions (*fufang* in Chinese). This was more complex than similar practices in many other parts of the world at that time. The Chinese language is not convenient enough to achieve precision in calculation. But mathematicians in China still excelled in their achievements. In the first century B.C. the Pythagoras Theorem was proposed in a Chinese Mathematics book. In the fifth century Chinese scientists had calculated the ratio of the circumference of a circle to its diameter to the seventh digit after the decimal point. China had also achieved a few major accomplishments in astronomy, in the invention of devices used for the prediction of earthquakes, and in her designs in various branches of engineering technology. For example, the earthquake-monitoring device, called the "*didongyi*" (地动仪, a seismograph), was the earliest device that could estimate the location of any earthquake. It was invented in 132 A.D. In the irrigation project, "*dujiangyan*"(都江堰), a weir was built in 256 B.C and it is still functioning today making a tremendous contribution as a dam.

❹ 中国 科技 的 发展
Zhōngguó kējì de fāzhǎn

可是 十 五 世纪 以后，中国 的 科技 却
Kěshì shí wǔ shìjì yǐhòu Zhōngguó de kējì què

落后 了。尤其 是 欧洲 用 安装 了 罗盘 的
luòhòu le Yóuqí shì Ōuzhōu yòng ānzhuāng le luópán de

船 来 到 中国，用 装上 火药 的 枪 炮 打败
chuán lái dào Zhōngguó yòng zhuāngshang huǒyào de qiāng pào dǎbài

中国，中国 人 觉得 自己 发明 的 东西，自己
Zhōngguó Zhōngguó rén juéde zìjǐ fāmíng de dōngxi zìjǐ

都 用 不 好。他们 对 自己 的 文明 失去
dōu yòng bù hǎo Tāmen duì zìjǐ de wénmíng shīqù

信心，不 认为 中国 是 个 善于 发明 的 国家。
xìnxīn bù rènwéi Zhōngguó shì gè shànyú fāmíng de guójiā

为什么 中国 会 落后，有 很 多 人 在
Wèishénme Zhōngguó huì luòhòu yǒu hěn duō rén zài

找 原因。有 人 说 是 因为 中国 一直 都 重视
zhǎo yuányīn Yǒu rén shuō shì yīnwèi Zhōngguó yīzhí dōu zhòngshì

农业、不 支持 工商业 发展，这 使 不 少
nóngyè bù zhīchí gōngshāngyè fāzhǎn zhè shǐ bù shǎo

科学 技术 没有 很 好 地 应用 和 推广。也
kēxué jìshù méiyǒu hěn hǎo de yìngyòng hé tuīguǎng Yě

有 人 认为 中国 的 很 多 技术 都 没有 深入[23]
Yǒu rén rènwéi Zhōngguó de hěn duō jìshù dōu méiyǒu shēnrù

研究，水平 不 高。但是，中国 的 科学家
yánjiū shuǐpíng bù gāo Dànshì Zhōngguó de kēxuéjiā

一直 在 努力 追赶[24] 世界 科技 发展 的 脚步。
yīzhí zài nǔlì zhuīgǎn shìjiè kējì fāzhǎn de jiǎobù

1965 年 中国 在 世界 上 首 次 人工[25]
nián Zhōngguó zài shìjiè shang shǒu cì réngōng

合成[26] 蛋白质[27]，获得 成功。被 称 为
héchéng dànbáizhì huòdé chénggōng Bèi chēng wéi

"杂交 水稻 之 父"的 袁 隆平，在 世界 上 第 一 次 成功 培植 出 杂交 水稻， 提高 了 粮食 的 产量。中国人 还 成功 研制²⁸ 出 原子弹²⁹、氢弹³⁰，成功 发射 人造 卫星³¹。 进入 二 十 一 世纪，中国 的 航天 飞机 终于 实现 了 载 人 上天 的 目标。但 当 你 明白 了 中国 科技 发展 的 历史，或许 你 会 更 明白，为什么 中国 实现 载 人 上 太空 后， 会 这么 高兴。现在 中国 的 科学 技术 仍然 不 算 先进，中国 要 有 能 与 祖先³² 相比 的 成就，还 要 继续 努力。

GLOSSARY

23	深入	go deep into	24	追赶	run after
25	人工	manual work	26	合成	compose
27	蛋白质	protein	28	研制	research and production of something
29	原子弹	atomic bomb	30	氢弹	hydrogen bomb
31	人造卫星	satellite	32	祖先	ancestor

Translation

❹ The Development of Chinese Technology

But after the fifteenth century the technology of China lagged behind her counterparts, especially when the Europeans used compass-equipped ships to sail to China and gunpowder-loaded guns to defeat the Chinese people, who had by then lost their confidence in their own civilization. They felt that they could not make good use of their own inventions and did not think China was a nation good at invention.

Why did China lag behind in development? Many people are trying to find answers. Some people have said that the reason was that China was concentrating on agriculture all the time and had not given enough support to industrial and commercial development. The above bias prevented quite a few further developments and the promotion of many fields in technology. Some people have claimed that in China many technological developments were of a relatively low level and the research was not deep and comprehensive enough. But in recent times scientists in China have been trying very hard all the time to catch up with the pace of development in many fields of technology in the world. In 1965 China showed to the world that she, for the first time, had succeeded in the synthesis of organic protein. Mr. Yuan Longping, who has been called "the father of hybridized paddy rice" is the first person in the world to crossbreed different species of paddy rice and has successfully produced a new hybridized paddy rice species, resulting in a boost in the production of food. Chinese people have also succeeded in the research and production of atomic bombs and hydrogen bombs, and have succeeded in launching satellites into space. Entering the twenty-first century, Chinese space shuttles finally have fulfilled the objective of sending people into space. After you have learned and understood the history of the development of science and technology in China maybe you will understand even better why the Chinese were so happy right after they had succeeded in sending someone into space. Up until now, the science and technology of China still cannot be regarded as very advanced. She still has to continue to work hard if she wants to achieve a high enough status so that modern day achievements can compare with those of the ancestors.

The use of acupuncture and moxibustion in treating diseases

Acupuncture and moxibustion are frequently used in various forms of therapies in traditional Chinese medicine. When carrying out the treatment method called "acupuncture", doctors use needles to insert into acupuncture points on the body to treat diseases. Doctors sometimes may use another method, called " moxibustion", in rendering treatments for diseases. The therapeutic effects of this method are achieved by the stimulation of the heat created by the burning of rolled up sticks of Chinese mugwort leaves. People sometimes combine the two treatment methods together and call the combined method, "acupunctural moxibustion".

Doctors of traditional Chinese medicine believe that many diseases can be treated successfully with "acupunctural moxibustion". The World Health Organization (WHO) has publicly announced that "acupunctural moxibustion" can actually have therapeutic effects on some diseases. People have also praised the effectiveness of "acupunctural moxibustion" in weight reduction and in the treatment of acne. Since this simple "acupunctural moxibustion" method could treat many diseases with good results as early as the Tang Dynasty, "acupunctural moxibustion" spread to Japan, Korea and some Arabian countries. Nowadays in Europe and America there are also quite a few people who use the "acupunctural moxibustion" method for therapeutic and cosmetic purposes.

GAMES FOR FUN

Among the following origins of things or events, which are the ones that resulted from the inventions of China?

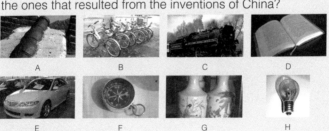

Zhōngguó de dà dūshì

中国的大都市

shì zěnyàng de

是怎样的？

How is Life in the Big Cities of China?

Pre-reading Questions

1. Why the train stations of China are crowded with a lot of people during Chinese New Year?

2. In your city, is there any similar case? Can you imagine the same problem is troubling the big cities of China?

3. The Chinese Government has been enforcing the policy of allowing only one child for each married couple. But if an extra baby was born, what would happen?

Zhōngguó de dūshìhuà

❶ 中国 的 都市化

jìn sān shí nián lái Zhōngguó shì shìjiè shang dūshìhuà[1]
近 三 十 年 来，中国 是 世界 上 都市化[1]

sùdù zuì kuài de guójiā zhī yī Gēnjù[2] tǒngjì[3] sān shí
速度 最 快 的 国家 之 一。根据[2] 统计[3]，三 十

nián lái Zhōngguó dàlù de dūshì rénkǒu zēngjiā le yì
年 来，中国 大陆 的 都市 人口 增加 了 4 亿。

Dào nián Zhōngguó de dūshì rénkǒu dàyuē yǒu yì
到 2006 年，中国 的 都市 人口 大约 有 5.7 亿，

zhàn le Zhōngguó rénkǒu de Dàn réngrán yǒu jìn yì
占 了 中国 人口 的 43.9%。但 仍然 有 近 8 亿

rén shēnghuó zài nóngcūn
人 生活 在 农村。

Zhōngguó dàlù bǎ rénkǒu fēn wéi chéngshì jūmín hé
中国 大陆 把 人口 分 为 城市 居民 和

nóngcūn jūmín Chéngshì hé nóngcūn de shēnghuó yǒu hěn dà de
农村 居民。城市 和 农村 的 生活 有 很 大 的

bùtóng Chéngshì jūmín zài chéngshì gōngzuò nóngcūn jūmín zhǐ
不同。城市 居民 在 城市 工作，农村 居民 只

néng zài nóngcūn gōngzuò Chéngshì jūmín de shōurù bǐ nóngcūn
能 在 农村 工作。城市 居民 的 收入 比 农村

jūmín gāo fúlì yě bǐ nóngcūn hǎo Dànshì chéngshì
居民 高，福利[4] 也 比 农村 好。但是，城市

de shēnghuó fèiyòng bǐ nóngcūn gāo Suǒyǐ chéngshì jūmín
的 生活 费用 比 农村 高。所以，城市 居民

The farming countryside of China

bù yuànyì duō shēng háizi Zài
不 愿意 多 生 孩子。在

nóngcūn rénmen shōurù jiào dī
农村，人们 收入 较 低，

fúlì shǎo Rénmen zhǐ néng duō
福利 少。人们 只 能 多

shēng háizi dāng fùmǔ lǎo
生 孩子，当 父母 老

le kěyǐ ràng háizi men yǎng
了，可以 让 孩子 们 养

huó fùmǔ
活 父母。

Chéngshì de fāzhǎn xūyào
城市 的 发展 需要

The peasant laborers who go to work in the cities

dàliàng láodònglì érqiě chéngshì shōurù gāo yúshì dàliàng
大量 劳动力[5]，而且 城市 收入 高，于是 大量

nóngcūn jūmín yǒng rù chéngshì
农村 居民 涌[6] 入 城市。

Měi nián chūnjié guò hòu zài gè
每 年 春节 过 后，在 各

gè chēzhàn dōu kěyǐ kàndào
个 车站，都 可以 看到

hěn duō nóngcūn jūmín zhǔnbèi dào
很 多 农村 居民 准备 到

chéngshì zhǎo gōngzuò Dàjiā jiào
城市 找 工作。大家 叫

tāmen zuò míngōng
他们 做 "民工"。

The high buildings of Shanghai

GLOSSARY

1 都市化 urbanization   2 根据 according to
3 统计 statistics   4 福利 welfare
5 劳动力 labor force   6 涌 surge into

Translation

❶ The Urbanization of China

Within the past 30 years China is one of the countries that has had the highest speed of urbanization. According to statistics within the afore-mentioned 30 years, the population of the cities in China has increased to the amount of four hundred million. In 2006 the urban population in China was about 5.7 hundred million, 43.9% of the total Chinese population, but there are close to eight hundred million people who are still living in the countryside.

The Chinese Government has categorized the Chinese population into two categories, urban residents and rural residents. There are big differences between urban life and city life. Urban residents have the rightful status to work in the cities, and, officially, rural residents can only work in the rural areas. The average income of urban residents is higher than that of rural residents. And the quality of their social welfare is better than that of rural residents. But the average cost of living in a city is higher than that of living in the countryside. Therefore, most urban residents are unwilling to have too many children. In the rural areas the average income is lower and the welfare services from the government are less than those in the cities. (Rural people can only "invest" into having more children as their retirement welfare.) When the parents get old, many children can better support their parents. This is a common attitude of the people in the countryside towards having more children.

The development of the cities requires a lot of labor. Therefore a lot of rural residents surge into the cities (trying to get jobs). Every year after the Spring Festival in every train station you can see a lot of rural residents getting ready to go to the cities to look for jobs. Everybody calls them mingong, literally meaning peasant laborers.

❷ 都市 人口 过 多引发 都市 问题

大量 人口 涌 入 都市，都市 人口 过
多，引发 了 许多 都市 问题。过多[7] 的 人 在
都市 生活，需要 吃饭，需要 用 水，需要 用
电，消耗[8] 了 大量 的 粮食[9] 和 能源[10]。

都市 人口 越来越 多，城市 也 越来越
拥挤[11]，居住 空间 越来越 小。在 香港、上海
这些 国际 大 都市 中，也 能 见 到 一 家

People are living in a crowded condition

几 口 人 挤 在 一 间
大约 只有 十 平方米 的
小屋子 里。

都市 的 汽车 越来越
多，马路 越来越 挤，
经常 会 塞车。在 一些
大 都市，例如 广州 的
公共汽车 上，常常 拥挤

de lián zhàn de wèizhi dōu méiyǒu
得 连 站 的 位置 都 没有。

Shàngbān zú de rén chángcháng bàoyuàn dūshì li rénqún
上班 族 的 人 常常 抱怨[12] 都市 里 人群

mìjí jiāotōng yōngjǐ Dūshì de shīyè zhě què kěwàng
密集，交通 拥挤。都市 的 失业 者 却 渴望

jiārù zhège rénqún Hěn duō rén yǒng rù dūshì zhǎo
加入 这个 人群。很 多 人 涌 入 都市 找

gōngzuò ér zhíwèi de shùliàng bùgòu gōngzuò jìngzhēng shífēn
工作，而 职位 的 数量 不够，工作 竞争 十分

jīliè Zài Běijīng Shànghǎi Guǎngzhōu zhèxiē dà dūshì zhōng
激烈[13]。在 北京、上海、广州 这些 大 都市 中，

dōu yǒu xǔduō zhǎo bù dào gōngzuò de wàidì rén
都 有 许多 找 不 到 工作 的 外地 人。

The busy traffic of the cities

Zài dūshì li gōngchǎng de jīqì shēng qìchē
在 都 市 里 ， 工 厂 的 机 器 声 、 汽 车

de lǎba shēng děng shǐ dūshì nányǐ ānjìng Gōngchǎng
的 喇 叭¹⁴ 声 等 ， 使 都 市 难 以 安 静 。 工 厂

de yāncōng qìchē de páiqìguǎn dōu pái chu dàliàng
的 烟 囱¹⁵ 、 汽 车 的 排 气 管¹⁶ 都 排 出 大 量

fèiqì Cóngqián běifāng gōngyè chéngshì Tàiyuán de tiānkōng
废 气¹⁷ 。 从 前 ， 北 方 工 业 城 市 太 原 的 天 空

chángcháng shì huīsè de Gōngchǎng pái chu de fèi shuǐ
常 常 是 灰 色 的 。 工 厂 排 出 的 废 水 ，

wūrǎn le héliú húpō Zhōngguó dōngběi de chéngshì
污 染 了 河 流 湖 泊 。 中 国 东 北 的 城 市

Hā'ěrbīn jiù céngjīng yīnwèi shuǐ wūrǎn ér yào tíng shuǐ
哈 尔 滨 就 曾 经 因 为 水 污 染¹⁸ 而 要 停 水

sì tiān
四 天 。

GLOSSARY

7	过多	excessive	8	消耗	use up
9	粮食	grain	10	能源	energy
11	拥挤	be crowded	12	抱怨	complain
13	激烈	fiercely	14	喇叭	car horns
15	烟囱	chimney	16	排气管	exhaust pipe
17	废气	pollutants in air	18	污染	pollution

Translation

❷ The Emergence of Urban Problems as a Result of Excessive Urban Population

As a result of a lot of people surging into the cities, the excessive pressure of overpopulation has led to many urban problems. More people living in the cities need more food, more water and more electricity. They consume a lot of food and energy.

As the size of the population in the urban areas becomes larger and larger, the various cities are getting more and more crowded and the average residential area is getting smaller and smaller. In large metropolitan cities like Hong Kong and Shanghai you can see quite a number of families, each with several members, squeezing into small houses with an average living area of about ten square meters.

As there are more and more cars in the cities, the roads are more and more crowded with them, resulting in frequent episodes of traffic congestion. In some big cities, Guangzhou for example, the public buses are frequently so crowded that even standing space is unavailable during rush hour.

Commuters naturally voice frequent complaints about the excessive population density and the congested traffic conditions of these large cities. Even so, the unemployed in those big cities are eager to join this group of commuters. Since there are a lot of people rushing into the cities looking for jobs, the competition to get employed is very keen. In large cities like Beijing, Shanghai and Guangzhou there are a lot of unemployed people who are migrants from other areas of China.

It is hard for a city to provide a nice and quiet lifestyle because of the amount of noise pollution from machines operating in the factories and from car horns, etc. A lot of pollutants are being emitted from factory chimneys, and the exhaust pipes of automobiles which are polluting the environment and causing air pollution. At one time the sky of the northern industrial city Taiyuan was frequently grey in color. The wastewater from factories has polluted rivers and lakes. Once, the water supply to the northeastern city Haerbin had to be suspended for four days because of water pollution.

❸ 都市人的压力
Dūshì rén de yālì

都市的生活比农村好，但压力[19]也
Dūshì de shēnghuó bǐ nóngcūn hǎo dàn yālì yě

很大。根据一些民间的统计，在北京、
hěn dà gēnjù yīxiē mínjiān de tǒngjì zài Běijīng

上海、广州等大都市，超过90%的都市人
Shànghǎi Guǎngzhōu děng dà dūshì chāoguò de dūshì rén

感到来自[20]工作和生活的压力。
gǎndào láizì gōngzuò hé shēnghuó de yālì

在私营企业[21]工作，好像永远有做不
zài sīyíng qǐyè gōngzuò hǎoxiàng yǒngyuǎn yǒu zuò bù

完的事。在一些公司或工厂，员工经常
wán de shì Zài yīxiē gōngsī huò gōngchǎng yuángōng jīngcháng

加班[22]，却没有相应的报酬。人们每个月
jiābān què méiyǒu xiāngyìng de bàochou Rénmen měi gè yuè

交了住房贷款[23]、汽车贷款、水电费以后，
jiāo le zhùfáng dàikuǎn qìchē dàikuǎn shuǐdiàn fèi yǐhòu

工资就已经剩下很少了。都市的工作
gōngzī jiù yǐjīng shèngxia hěn shǎo le Dūshì de gōngzuò

竞争很激烈，人们常常担心自己会失业[24]
jìngzhēng hěn jīliè rénmen chángcháng dānxīn zìjǐ huì shīyè

在中国大陆，到现在为止，在大型
Zài Zhōngguó dàlù dào xiànzài wéizhǐ zài dàxíng

国有企业[25]里工作还算不错。工作比较
guóyǒu qǐyè li gōngzuò hái suàn bùcuò gōngzuò bǐjiào

轻松，收入不错，失业的压力比较小。为
qīngsōng shōurù bùcuò shīyè de yālì bǐjiào xiǎo Wèi

政府工作的公务员退休后可以领取
zhèngfǔ gōngzuò de gōngwùyuán tuìxiū hòu kěyǐ lǐng qǔ

退休金[26]，国家还为他们的生活和健康
tuìxiūjīn guójiā hái wèi tāmen de shēnghuó hé jiànkāng

提供 帮助。但是，想 进入 大型 国有 企业 工作，或者 当 公务员，必须 通过 很 多 严格²⁷的 考试，这 也 不 是 一 件 容易 的 事情。

都市 人 生活 在 工作 压力 和 生活 压力 下，容易 出现 健康 问题。2006 年 的 一 项 调查 显示，中国90%以上 的 都市 人 都 有 不同 的 健康 问题。十 个 年轻 职员 中，就 有 两人 的 肝脏²⁸患病。工作 和 生活 的 压力 使 人 精神 紧张，容易 引发 心理²⁹问题，甚至 自杀。在 中国，15 到 34 岁 的 人群 最 主要 的 死因 是 自杀³⁰。

GLOSSARY

19	压力	pressure	20	来自 come from
21	私营企业	private enterprise	22	加班 work overtime
23	贷款	loan	24	失业 unemployed
25	国有企业	state enterprise	26	退休金 retirement payment
27	严格	strict	28	肝脏 liver
29	心理	psychological	30	自杀 commit suicide

Translation

❸ The Pressures Experienced by People Living in the Cities

The quality of life in the urban areas is better than in the rural areas. But the pressures of living in a city are very high too. From some unofficial statistics gathered casually from people's subjective opinions, 90% of the population living in big cities like Beijing, Shanghai and Guangzhou claim that they feel the pressures from work and from the urban way of life.

Workers employed in private companies seem to be given jobs which they can never finish. In some companies and factories, employees frequently have to work overtime without receiving their entitled extra payment for the extra workload. Every month after paying the rent or mortgage of their home, the monthly car installment, and the water and electricity bill payments, people find that there is very little left from their salaries. The competition to keep one's job in the city is very keen. People frequently worry about losing their job and becoming unemployed.

Up to this time, being employed by the large-scale government-owned enterprises is still regarded as having quite a good status. The working environment and the workload are relatively more relaxed in nature. The average income is not bad too, and the pressure of losing one's job is relatively less. After retirement, government employees in the public services can also receive a monthly retirement payment. The state also provides support services for them to lead a better and healthier life. But it is not easy to get a job in the large-scale state-owned enterprises or to become a government officer. These individuals have to pass a lot of strict examinations before they get these good jobs.

Urban citizens living under the combined effect of pressures from work and urban life are more likely to be troubled by health-related problems. One of the statistics in 2006 has revealed that in China over 90% of the urban residents have various health problems. For each ten young workers there are two suffering from liver disease of different causes. The combined effect of pressures from work and urban life makes people tense and nervous mentally. They are more susceptible to psychiatric problems. Some of them even commit suicide. In China, the main cause of death of people in the age group 15 to 34 is suicide.

The policy of a single child per each married couple

Since 1949 the population in China has been increasing rapidly. Overpopulation has led to many serious problems. Concrete examples of these problems are: problems resulting from the large amount of energy needed for consumption, the lack of housing, the increase in pressure for students to find a vacancy for them to continue their education, the keen competition to get employment, difficulties in managing the rapidly increasing population and the environmental damage which is a result of this rapid increase. Under these circumstances the Chinese Government cannot afford not to put in a long-term family planning policy to control the rate of population increase.

Since 1979 the Chinese Government has put in a long-term family planning policy. Some people do not fully understand the exact terms under this policy and think that under this family planning policy all Chinese families can only have one child per married couple. In actual fact, according to the regulations of the Chinese Government it is only in the cities that the majority of the families can only have one child per married couple. If both people in a married couple were born as a single child of their parents, this couple can give birth to two children. In the rural areas every family is entitled to the right to give birth to two children.

In the western part of China where a lot of ethnic minorities live, each family can have several children. If people have violated the rules and regulations of this family-planning policy and have given birth to an extra baby, they are subject to pay a fine.

For many years the Chinese Government has been controlling the amount of the population, and the rate of increase is obviously slowing down.

According to estimates, without the Chinese Government's inauguration of the above family-planning policy, the population of China could be 3 billion more than the present figure!

GAMES FOR FUN

Congratulations! You have obtained residential status for living in China. First please fill in this pamphlet for recording the information of each household (户口本)!

常住人口登记卡

姓名		户主或与 户主关系			
曾用名		性别			
出生地		民族			
籍贯		出生日期			
本市（县）住址			宗教信仰		
公民身份证件编号		身高		血型	
文化程度		婚姻状况		兵役情况	
服务处所				职业	
何时由何地迁来本市（县）					
何时由何地迁来本址					

Notes:
户主   means house holder.
文化程度   means your education background.
服务处所   means the company you are working in.

Zhōngguó rén dōu shuō yī yàng de yǔ yán

中国人都说一样的语言，

xiě yī yàng de zì ma

写一样的字吗？

Do all Chinese people speak the same language and write the same kind of Chinese characters?

Pre-reading Questions

1. In China, why can't the northern people understand the language of the southern people?

2. Why do the Chinese people speaking different dialects write the same Chinese characters?

3. Some Chinese calligraphic art pieces look like linear pictures. Can Chinese people really understand what they mean?

Zhōngguó rén shuō de yǔyán

❶ 中国人说的语言

Zhōngguó yǒu wǔ shí liù gè mínzú yīgòng yǒu

中国 有 五 十 六 个 民族，一共 有

bāshíduōzhǒng yǔyán sān shí zhǒng wénzì Zuì zhǔyào de

八十多种 语言，三 十 种 文字。最 主要 的

yǔyán hé wénzì chēng wéi Zhōngwén yě jiùshì Hànyǔ hé

语言 和 文字 称 为 中文，也 就是 汉语 和

Hànzì

汉字。

Hànyǔ shì hěn gǔlǎo[1] de yǔyán yě shì shìjiè

汉语 是 很 古老[1] 的 语言，也 是 世界

shang shǐyòng rénshù zuì duō de yǔyán Quán guó tōngyòng² de
上 使用 人数 最 多 的 语言。全 国 通用² 的

Hànyǔ yǐ Běijīng yǔyīn wéi biāozhǔn³ yīn zài Zhōngguó
汉语，以 北京 语音 为 标准³ 音，在 中国

dàlù jiàozuò Pǔtōnghuà zài Táiwān jiàozuò guóyǔ zhè shì
大陆 叫做 普通话，在 台湾 叫做 国语，这 是

Zhōngguó gè gè mínzú gòngtóng shǐyòng de yǔyán Zhōngguó hěn
中国 各 个 民族 共同 使用 的 语言。中国 很

dà gè gè dìfang de rén shuō de Hànyǔ fāyīn⁴ hé
大，各 个 地方 的 人 说 的 汉语，发音⁴ 和

cíyǔ dōu yǒu xiē bù yīyàng zhè jiùshì fāngyán⁵ fāngyán
词语 都 有 些 不 一样，这 就是 方言⁵，方言

yě jiàozuò dìfāng huà tā zhǐ zài mǒu yī gè dìqū
也 叫做 地方 话，它 只 在 某 一 个 地区

shǐyòng Qítā dìqū de rén shì tīng bù míngbai de
使用。其他 地区 的 人 是 听 不 明白 的。

Xiàng Xiānggǎngrén jiǎng Guǎngdōng huà⁶ Táiwān rén jiǎng Mǐn nán huà⁷
像 香港人 讲 广东 话⁶、台湾 人 讲 闽南 话⁷，

jiùshì jiǎng fāngyán Hěn duō zài wàiguó zhù de huáqiáo yě
就是 讲 方言。很 多 在 外国 住 的 华侨 也

shì jiǎng fāngyán
是 讲 方言。

GLOSSARY

1 古老 ancient
2 通用 in common use
3 标准 standard
4 发音 pronounce
5 方言 dialect
6 广东话 Cantonese
7 闽南话 Fukienese

Translation

❶ The languages spoken by Chinese people

China has 56 ethnic tribes. There are over 80 languages and 30 kinds of written words. The main one that is most commonly used is the Chinese language and the system of written words, called Zhongwen, which is also called Hanyu (the language of the Han) and Hanzi (the written words of the Han).

Hanyu is a very old language and is also the language used by the largest number of people in the world. The pronunciation of HanYu, which is in use by people all over China, is standardized according to the Beijing dialect. In China hanyu is called putongtua and in Taiwan it is called Mandarin. This is the common language used by all the ethnic tribes in China. China is a very big country and the hanyu spoken by people of different regions may have different ways of pronunciation and different ways of expression. These variants of hanyu are called dialects, which are also called regional dialects. The use of each dialect is confined to one region. People from other regions cannot comprehend what is being said in dialects other than theirs. People in Hong Kong speak Cantonese (广东话, Guangdonghua) and people in Taiwan speak Fukienese (闽南话, Minnamhua). Many overseas Chinese who live in foreign countries also speak different dialects.

Zhōngguó de wénzì　　Hànzì

❷ 中国 的 文字 —— 汉字

Zhōngguórén xiě de wénzì zhǔyào shì Hànzì
中国人 写 的 文字 主要 是 汉字。

Wèishénme Zhōngguórén jiǎng fāngyán shí hùxiāng tīng bù dǒng
为什么 中国人 讲 方言 时 互相 听 不 懂,

què xiě yīyàng de wénzì ne Yīnwèi èrqiānduōnián qián
却 写 一样 的 文字 呢? 因为 二千多年 前,

Zhōngguó dìyī gè huángdì Qínshǐhuáng mìnglìng tǒngyī wénzì
中国 第一 个 皇帝 秦始皇 命令 统一 [8] 文字,

tā hěn róngyì jiù bàn dào le Qínshǐhuáng méiyǒu tǒngyī
他 很 容易 就 办 到 了。秦始皇 没有 统一

yǔyán Tǒngyī yǔyán shì èr shí
语言。 统一 语言 是 二 十

shìjì de shì bǐ tǒngyī wénzì
世纪 的 事, 比 统一 文字

wǎn de duō le Wèi tǒngyī yǔyán
晚 得 多 了。未 统一 语言

月 —— moon

zhīqián Zhōngguórén tīng bù dǒng duìfāng
之前,中国人 听 不 懂 对方

zài shuō shénme de shíhou huì
在 说 什么 的 时候, 会

ná chū bǐ lai xiě zhàoyàng néng
拿 出 笔 来 写,照样 能

大 —— big

jiāo péngyou Dāngshí Zhōngguórén hé
交 朋友。 当时 中国人 和

Rìběnrén Hánguórén yě nénggòu bǐ
日本人、韩国人 也 能够 笔

tán hùxiāng liǎojiě ne
谈,互相 了解 呢。

Hànzì shì bu shì hěn nán xué
汉字 是 不 是 很 难 学

雨 —— rain

呢？汉字 是 表示 意思 的，不 是 拼音文字。

初 学 的 人 不 知道 它 怎么 读 和 写，

觉得 很 难。其实 汉字 也 有 组成 规律[9]。

对 不 认识 的 字，仔细 看看，你 会 发现

有些 部分 可能 已经 学 过。汉字 的 组成

就 像 砌 积木 的 游戏。每 个 汉字 方方[10]

的，看 起来 很 整齐[11]。用 汉字 还 能够 玩

很多 文字 游戏 呢，例如 绕口令，成语

接龙 等等。

GLOSSARY

8 统一 unify

9 规律 rule; regularity

10 方 square

11 整齐 neat

Translation

❷ The Written Words of China — Hanzi, Chinese Characters

The written language of the Chinese people is written mainly in Chinese characters, called hanzis. The Chinese cannot understand each other when they speak their own dialects, but why they write the same characters? The reason is that over 2000 years ago the first Emperor of China, Qinshihuang ordered the unification of all the written languages (using the system of hanzis as the only written language). (Being a dictator) He did that easily. Qinshihuang did not order the unification of all the spoken languages. It was in the twentieth century that China tried to unify all the spoken languages of the Chinese people. This attempt of unification of the spoken languages happened a lot later than the unification of the written language. Before the completion of the unification of all the spoken languages in China and when people who had the knowledge of hanzis, people could take out their pens and communicate by writing out what they wanted to say in Hanzis. People could make new friends that way. During that period of time Chinese, Japanese and Koreans could understand one another by writing Hanzis as a form of communication, just like pen pals.

Are Hanzis difficult to learn? Hanzis are pictorial symbols for words and phrases. They are not phonetic symbols (like those words and phrases in English). Beginners who do not know how to read and write so many of them may find learning them very difficult. As a matter of fact the composition of Hanzis also has its rules and regularities. If you look carefully at the Hanzis, (which you cannot recognize you may discover that) some parts of them you might have learned before. The composition of Hanzis is like a jigsaw puzzle. Every Hanzi is like a small square and it looks very neat and regular. Hanzis can be used to play a lot of games of words too, like tongue twisters and the game of proverb fan-tan (the linking up of the end of a proverb with the beginning of another proverb when the end word and the beginning word of the two proverbs are the same Hanzis).

❸ <ruby>中国<rt>Zhōngguó</rt></ruby> <ruby>书法<rt>shūfǎ</rt></ruby> <ruby>是<rt>shì</rt></ruby> <ruby>文字<rt>wénzì</rt></ruby> <ruby>还是<rt>háishi</rt></ruby> <ruby>图画<rt>túhuà</rt></ruby>？

<ruby>将<rt>Jiāng</rt></ruby> <ruby>文字<rt>wénzì</rt></ruby> <ruby>写<rt>xiě</rt></ruby> <ruby>得<rt>de</rt></ruby> <ruby>好<rt>hǎo</rt></ruby> <ruby>看<rt>kàn</rt></ruby>，<ruby>是<rt>shì</rt></ruby> <ruby>书法<rt>shūfǎ</rt></ruby>[12] <ruby>的<rt>de</rt></ruby> <ruby>艺术<rt>yìshù</rt></ruby>。<ruby>谈<rt>Tán</rt></ruby> <ruby>西方<rt>xīfāng</rt></ruby> <ruby>艺术<rt>yìshù</rt></ruby>，<ruby>很<rt>hěn</rt></ruby> <ruby>少<rt>shǎo</rt></ruby> <ruby>谈<rt>tán</rt></ruby> <ruby>书法<rt>shūfǎ</rt></ruby>；<ruby>谈<rt>tán</rt></ruby> <ruby>中国<rt>Zhōngguó</rt></ruby> <ruby>艺术<rt>yìshù</rt></ruby>，<ruby>却<rt>què</rt></ruby> <ruby>不能不<rt>bùnéngbù</rt></ruby> <ruby>谈<rt>tán</rt></ruby> <ruby>书法<rt>shūfǎ</rt></ruby>。<ruby>中国<rt>Zhōngguó</rt></ruby> <ruby>书法<rt>shūfǎ</rt></ruby> <ruby>的<rt>de</rt></ruby> <ruby>特色<rt>tèsè</rt></ruby>，<ruby>与<rt>yǔ</rt></ruby> <ruby>汉字<rt>Hànzì</rt></ruby> <ruby>的<rt>de</rt></ruby> <ruby>特点<rt>tèdiǎn</rt></ruby> <ruby>和<rt>hé</rt></ruby> <ruby>书写<rt>shūxiě</rt></ruby> <ruby>工具<rt>gōngjù</rt></ruby> <ruby>有<rt>yǒu</rt></ruby> <ruby>密切<rt>mìqiè</rt></ruby>[13] <ruby>的<rt>de</rt></ruby> <ruby>关系<rt>guānxi</rt></ruby>。

<ruby>欣赏<rt>Xīnshǎng</rt></ruby> <ruby>中国<rt>Zhōngguó</rt></ruby> <ruby>书法<rt>shūfǎ</rt></ruby> <ruby>时<rt>shí</rt></ruby>，<ruby>中国人<rt>Zhōngguórén</rt></ruby> <ruby>也<rt>yě</rt></ruby> <ruby>未必<rt>wèibì</rt></ruby> <ruby>能<rt>néng</rt></ruby> <ruby>完全<rt>wánquán</rt></ruby> <ruby>认<rt>rèn</rt></ruby> <ruby>出<rt>chū</rt></ruby> <ruby>当中<rt>dāngzhōng</rt></ruby> <ruby>的<rt>de</rt></ruby> <ruby>汉字<rt>Hànzì</rt></ruby>。<ruby>因为<rt>Yīnwèi</rt></ruby> <ruby>从<rt>cóng</rt></ruby> <ruby>古<rt>gǔ</rt></ruby> <ruby>至<rt>zhì</rt></ruby> <ruby>今<rt>jīn</rt></ruby>，<ruby>汉字<rt>Hànzì</rt></ruby> <ruby>字体<rt>zìtǐ</rt></ruby>[14] <ruby>一直<rt>yīzhí</rt></ruby> <ruby>在<rt>zài</rt></ruby> <ruby>变<rt>biàn</rt></ruby>，<ruby>有些<rt>yǒuxiē</rt></ruby> <ruby>现在<rt>xiànzài</rt></ruby> <ruby>已<rt>yǐ</rt></ruby> <ruby>不<rt>bù</rt></ruby> <ruby>再<rt>zài</rt></ruby> <ruby>使用<rt>shǐyòng</rt></ruby>，<ruby>但<rt>dàn</rt></ruby> <ruby>仍然<rt>réngrán</rt></ruby> <ruby>出现<rt>chūxiàn</rt></ruby> <ruby>在<rt>zài</rt></ruby> <ruby>书法<rt>shūfǎ</rt></ruby> <ruby>作品<rt>zuòpǐn</rt></ruby>

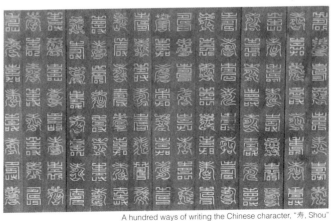

A hundred ways of writing the Chinese character, "寿, Shou"

The Seal Character

The Li Shu, an ancient style of calligraphy current in the Han Dynasty

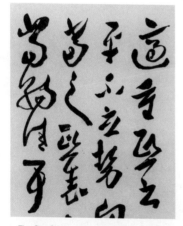

The Cao Shu, a cursive style of calligraphy

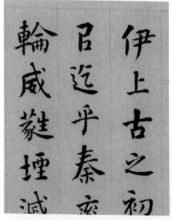

The Kai Shu, the regular script of calligraphy

zhōng　Jù　tánxìng　de　máobǐ　diǎn shang mò hòu kěyǐ
中。具　弹性[15]　的　毛笔，点　上　墨　后，可以

huà　chu　cūyòu　shēnqiǎn　bùtóng　de　xiàntiáo　biǎoxiàn
画　出　粗幼、深浅　不同　的　线条，表现

bùtóng　zìtǐ　de　měi　zhuànshū　xiàntiáo　cūyòu　jūnyún
不同　字体　的　美：篆书[16]　线条　粗幼　均匀[17]，

有 稳重[18] 的 感觉；隶书[19] 线条 轻重 变化
大，表现 力量；草书[20] 线条 有 动感[21]，表现
活力；楷书[22] 是 今天 常见 的 字体，线条
有 细致[23] 变化，有 灵巧[24] 的 感觉。

与 拼音 文字 不同，因为 汉字 不
是 由 少量 字母 重复 组合 而 成，
而 是 每 个 字 都 各 有 独特[25] 的 形状。

书法 中 的 汉字，有 大小、形状、粗幼、
深浅 不同 的 变化，既 是 文字，又 像
图画。即使[26] 你 未 能够 看 明白 中国 书法
的 内容，也 可以 试 试 欣赏[27] 当中 的 美。

GLOSSARY

12	书法	calligraphy		13	密切	close
14	字体	script		15	弹性	flexible; elasticity
16	篆书	seal script		17	均匀	even
18	稳重	steady		19	隶书	clerical script
20	草书	cursive script		21	动感	dynamic; vivid
22	楷书	regular script		23	细致	fine
24	灵巧	dexterous		25	独特	unique
26	即使	even though		27	欣赏	appreciate

Translation

❸ Is Chinese calligraphy an expression of words or is it an expression of pictures?

The art of calligraphy is to write the words in a beautiful manner. When people talk about Western art they seldom talk about the calligraphy of European languages. When we talk about Chinese art we can never avoid talking about Chinese calligraphy, the special feature of which is closely related to the special characteristics of hanzis and the tools for writing them.

When Chinese people appreciate Chinese calligraphy they may not be able to recognize all the Chinese characters written in that particular piece of Chinese calligraphy because from ancient times till now the ways of writing different forms of Hanzis are changing all the time. Some of the forms are no longer in use in the written language and yet they might appear here and there among art pieces of Chinese calligraphy. The highly flexible paint brush after being soaked in black ink can draw and paint different kinds of lines, from thick ones to thin ones and from dark shades of black to light shades of black. Different compositions can express different forms of the beauty of different scripts. The lines forming the seal scripts are regularly equal in thickness, making people feel their stability. The lines composing the clerical scripts vary greatly in lightness and heaviness, making people feel their strength. The cursive scripts in Chinese calligraphy appears very vivid, making people feel its energy. The regular scripts are the most commonly used in today's writing. The lines composing them are fine and full of minute variations, making people feel their dexterity.

Chinese Hanzis differ from phonetic words because they are not formed from repetitive compositions of a small number of alphabets and each hanzi has its special and unique shape. The Hanzis in Chinese calligraphy vary in sizes, in shapes, in thickness and different shades of black color of the lines. They are written words as well as pictures. Even though you may not be able to understand the contents in Chinese calligraphy you can at least appreciate its beauty.

What are the differences between simplified Chinese characters and traditional Chinese characters?

The Chinese characters that we are using now can be differentiated into the traditional scripts and the simplified scripts, (two versions of Chinese characters). In a comparatively more complete manner the traditional scripts version keeps the shapes and the meanings of the Chinese characters that have been in use from ancient time till now. The simplified version is based on the simplification of the Chinese characters of the traditional version. The majority of the shapes of the traditional Chinese characters have been simplified and some of characters have changes of meaning. Let's take the examples of the two simplified Chinese characters, "马" (pronounced as Ma, meaning a horse), and "后" ,(pronounced as Hou, meaning behind in the simplified and a queen both in the traditional version and simplified version). The Chinese character, "馬" (pronounced as Ma, meaning a horse) in the traditional version has become "马" after it is converted into the simplified version. The shape has been simplified but the original meaning has been kept, unchanged. But both of the Chinese characters, "后" , (pronounced as Hou meaning a queen) and "後" , (pronounced as Hou meaning behind in the context of time in one occasion and space in another occasion)"in the traditional version have become the same Chinese character, "后" in the simplified version. When the Chinese character "後" of the traditional version has been simplified as "后" in the simplified version, not only has the shape been simplified, the meaning too has been altered (because it carries a double meaning as one simplified Chinese character. It can mean behind in the context of time or space. It can also mean a queen when it is used as a noun.)

The simplified version of Chinese characters is developed from the traditional version of Chinese characters, which are composed of many strokes, making them difficult to write and difficult to be recognized. In order to popularize culture linguists of Mainland China in the beginning of the 20th century suggested the adoption and popularization of the simplified version of Chinese characters. Now in Mainland China the simplified version of Chinese characters is being used throughout the mainland. In Taiwan (China), Hong Kong and Macau (two special administrative regions of China) the traditional version of Chinese characters is being used. Outside of China different places make different choices regarding which version to use. For example the Chinese in Malaysia use the simplified version of Chinese characters. In Thailand the traditional version of Chinese characters is being used. Both the simplified version and the traditional version have their advantages. Simplified Chinese characters are easier to write and easier to be recognized. Many foreign beginning learners of the Chinese language like to start with the studying of the simplified version of Chinese characters. But the traditional version of Chinese characters can be better and more completely keep the Chinese characters' meanings, which have a long-standing and well-established history of usages. Therefore it is easier to guess the meaning of a Chinese character from its shape when a student is studying Chinese with the use of the traditional version of Chinese characters. If someone wants to take an advanced step in the study and research of the Chinese language he or she must learn the traditional version of Chinese characters. Therefore in Mainland China, the students who major in the study of the Chinese language have to learn the traditional version of Chinese characters too.

GAMES FOR FUN

The following Chinese characters are the ancient version of Chinese characters. From their shapes can you guess what are they individually?

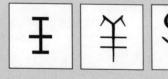

—— —— —— —— ——

王 羊 子 耳 八
Answers:

Zhōngguó rén zěn yàng kàn zìrán

中国人怎样看自然？

How do Chinese People Look at Nature?

Pre-reading Questions

1. Why do Chinese people paint picture in such a format of long and rolled up scroll? Isn't it inconvenient to look at these pictures gradually bit by bit as they have to be slowly unrolled?

2. If you were a landscape garden designer and a client from China asked you to design a large Chinese garden, what design would you set?

3. If you are going to select things from Nature to represent separation, love and purity what will you select? What do you think Chinese people will select?

Gēn huàjiā yītóng yóu shān wán shuǐ

❶ 跟 画家 一同 游 山 玩 水

Xiǎngxiàng yī xià zài qiūrì de lántiān xià nǐ
想像 一 下 ， 在 秋日[1] 的 蓝天 下 ， 你

yán zhe jiāng biān sànbù Bù yuǎn de duì'àn yǒu jǐ zuò
沿 着 江 边 散步[2]。 不 远 的 对岸[3]， 有 几 座

xiǎo shān Zǒu zhe zǒu zhe yǎnqián chūxiàn le yī dà piàn
小 山。 走 着 走 着 ， 眼前 出现 了 一 大 片

shānpō Nǐ yībiān pá shang shān yībiān xīnshǎng lù biān de
山坡。 你 一边 爬 上 山 ， 一边 欣赏 路 边 的

怪石 和 大树。终于 到达 山顶 了，从 高处
向 下 望：不 远 处 的 山 上 有 片 树林，林
中 有 小 屋、凉亭。再 望 向 远方，水 中 有
一 只 小 船，还 有 人 在 船 上 钓鱼 呢。你
很 想 游览[4] 这么 动人 的 地方 吧？原来 只要
看看 著名 的 中国 山水 画——《富春 山 居
图》（创作 于 公元 十 四 世纪），你 就 可以
跟 着 画家 走 进 画 中，一同 游 山 玩 水[5]。

西方 也 有 风景 画。西方 的 风景
画 以 描写[6] 自然 的 面貌 为主。你 好像
和 画家 站 在 一起，看 着 一 片 静止[7] 的
风景。看 中国 的 山水 画[8]，尤其 是 长

Fuchun Shan Ju Tu (A painting of the life at Mountain Fuchun Area)

卷画，你可以从画的一边走进大
自然中，慢慢游览。到画卷的末端[9]，
你就从画中的大自然走出来，
回到真的世界中。在画中，你和动物、
花草、昆虫一样，都是大自然的
一部分。中国画不讲求真实地描写大
自然，而是希望看画的人在画中进入
自然，用心去感受自然的美。

GLOSSARY

1 秋日 autumn day 2 散步 take a walk
3 对岸 the opposite bank 4 游览 go sightseeing
5 游山玩水 enjoy the sights of mountains and rivers
6 描写 describe 7 静止 static
8 山水画 landscape painting 9 末端 the end

Translation

❶ To Travel and Enjoy the sights of Mountains and Rivers with the Painters

Imagine yourself strolling along the riverside under the blue sky of the autumn sun. Not too far away on the opposite side of the river there are a few small hills. While walking along a large stretch of hills, a slope appears right in front of your eyes. While you are climbing up the slope you are also appreciating the roadside pieces of stone with strange shapes and there are also large trees. Finally you have reached the hilltop and from high up there you look down. Not too far away there is a mountain with a forest, in which there is a small house and a pavilion. Then you look further and you see a small boat on the water. There is also someone fishing from that boat. Do you want to visit a place so inviting and so appealing? As a matter of fact you can do so by looking at a famous Chinese landscape painting, "Fuchun Shan Ju Tu" (富春山居图) , the picture of a mountain residence in Mount Fu Chun (painted in the 14th century B.C.). Then you can follow the artist to go inside the picture to travel high and low and enjoy the sights of mountains and rivers with the painters.

In the West there are also landscape paintings, which mainly portray the various scenic features of nature. It is like that you are standing together with the painter to look at static but beautiful scenery. When you look at Chinese landscape paintings, especially the picture scroll you can enter from one end of the painting to enter its world of the Nature and slowly stroll along until you reach the other end and come out from the Nature of the painting and go back into the real world. In the painting you are together with the animals, the flowers, the grass, and the insects which are all part of the Nature. Chinese paintings are not particular about the real portrayal of the Nature. Painters hope that people who appreciate their paintings can enter Nature and use their hearts to feel the beauty of Nature.

❷ 我的家就是大自然

你去过纽约大都会博物馆里的中国花园吗？这个花园是模仿[10]中国的苏州园林建造的。苏州是中国南方的著名城市。从前很多有钱人住在苏州，他们的房子有美丽的花园。园林就是花园的意思。现在这些苏州园林都成了著名旅游景点[11]。

在园林中，你会见到很多奇怪的石头。那些石头叠在一起，像一座座小山，这些小山叫做"假山"。假山上有亭子[12]；还有人造的小瀑布。园林里种了许多花和树，一年四季都有不同的花陪伴你。住在这里，你一定不会觉得寂寞[13]。你能听到鸟叫，看到蝴蝶飞舞，欣赏金鱼在池塘里自在地

yóu Dàole wǎnshang nǐ hái
游。到了 晚上，你 还

kěyǐ zuò zài tíngzi li
可以 坐 在 亭子 里

xīnshǎng yuèliang hé xīngxing
欣赏 月亮 和 星星。

Zhōngguórén bǎ zhěng gè dà
中国人 把 整 个 大

zìrán dōu bān dào zìjǐ
自然，都 搬 到 自己

jiā li
家 里。

A famous Suzhou garden — Zhuozheng Yuan (1)

Zài zhèyàng de jiā
　　在 这样 的 家

li shēnghuó rén yǔ zìrán
里 生活，人 与 自然

tèbié qīnjìn Nǐ huì wàngjì
特别 亲近。你 会 忘记

zìjǐ shì shēnghuó zài chéngshì
自己 是 生活 在 城市

A famous Suzhou garden — Zhuozheng Yuan (2)

li ér juéde hǎoxiàng shēnghuó zài níngjìng de dà zìrán
里，而 觉得 好像 生活 在 宁静 的 大 自然

zhōng Yuánlín li de jǐngsè bù zhǐshì mófǎng dà zìrán
中。园林 里 的 景色 不 只是 模仿 大 自然，

háishi měihuà le de dà zìrán Wúlùn zhàn zhe huòzhě
还是 美化¹⁴了 的 大 自然。无论 站 着 或者

sànbù nǐ dōu huì kàndào měilì de huàmiàn
散步，你 都 会 看到 美丽 的 画面。

GLOSSARY

10 模仿 imitate　　11 景点 scenic viewpoints for tourism
12 亭子 pavilion　　13 寂寞 lonely　　14 美化 beautify

Translation

❷ My home is the Great Nature

Have you been to the Chinese Garden in the New York Metropolitan Museum? This garden is an imitation construction of the Chinese Suzhou gardens. Suzhou is a famous Chinese city in the south. Some time ago there were a lot of rich people living in Suzhou and their houses had beautiful flower gardens, called "yuanlin", which means a garden. Now these gardens have become famous scenic viewpoints for tourism.

In these gardens you can see a lot of strange looking pieces of stone, being stacked together like many small hills, which are called "jiashan, fake hills". On these fake hills there are pavilions and even small artificial waterfalls. In these gardens there are a lot of flowers and trees. There are flowers throughout the four seasons of the year to accompany you. When you live here you will never feel lonely. You can hear birds singing, see butterflies flying around. You can appreciate how the gold fish swim comfortably in the fishpond. At night you can sit in the pavilion to appreciate the moon and the stars. Chinese people bring the whole Great Nature back to their own homes.

When you are living in a home with this kind of lifestyle you will feel that people and Nature are especially close together. You will forget that you are living in the city and you feel that you are living in the peaceful Great Nature. Not only is the scenery of the garden an imitation of the Great Nature but it also is a beautification of the Great Nature. No matter whether you are standing or strolling you will see scenes of beautiful pictures.

❸ Shī zhōng de fēnghuāxuěyuè
诗中的风花雪月

Zhōngguó rén rè'ài dà zìrán。Hěn duō Zhōngguó
中国 人 热爱 大 自然。很 多 中国

shīrén dōu zài shīgē zhōng miáoxiě dà zìrán, zànměi
诗人 都 在 诗歌 中 描写 大 自然,赞美 [15]

dà zìrán。Zhōngguó yǒu dàliàng miáoxiě shān hé huā
大 自然。中国 有 大量 描写 山、河、花、

shù děng zìrán jǐngwù de shānshuǐ shī hái yǒu hěn duō
树 等 自然 景物 的 山水 诗,还 有 很 多

miáoxiě tiányuán fēngguāng de tiányuán shī。Nǐ dú nàxiē
描写 田园 风光 的 田园 诗。你 读 那些

yōuměi de shījù jiù huì juéde hǎoxiàng jìnrù le shī
优美 的 诗句,就 会 觉得 好像 进入 了 诗

zhōng miáoxiě de fēngjǐng zhōng
中 描写 的 风景 中。

Zhōngguó shīrén yòng miáoxiě zìrán jǐngwù de fāngfǎ
中国 诗人 用 描写 自然 景物 的 方法,

lái biǎodá zìjǐ de gǎnqíng。Zài Zhōngguó shīgē zhōng
来 表达 自己 的 感情。在 中国 诗歌 中,

zìrán jǐngwù xiàng rén yīyàng yǒu kuàilè hé yōuchóu
自然 景物 像 人 一样 有 快乐 和 忧愁 [16]。

Shīrén kuàilè de shíhou shīgē zhōng de fēng yěshì
诗人 快乐 的 时候,诗歌 中 的 风 也是

yúkuài de。Shīrén shāngxīn de
愉快 的。诗人 伤心 的

shíhou shīgē zhōng de huā yě
时候,诗歌 中 的 花 也

zài kūqì
在 哭泣。

Zhōngguó shīgē zhōng de
中国 诗歌 中 的

The cold-weather-resistant plum blossom

自然 景物，还 常常 具有 特殊[17] 的 含义。
例如，诗歌 中 的 月亮，常常 表达 了 诗人
对 亲人、朋友 或 家乡 的 思念。诗人
舍不得 和 朋友 分别 时，常常 在 诗歌 中
写 柳树[18]，表达 不 想 分离[19] 的 感情。诗人
描写 梅花 不 怕 寒冷，是 为了 赞美 像
梅花 一样 坚强 的 人。西方 诗歌 常常 用
红 玫瑰 表示 爱情，中国 诗歌 表示 爱情
却 用 红豆[20] 或者 桃花。百合 花 在 西方
诗歌 中 代表 纯洁，中国 诗歌 会 用 莲花。

GLOSSARY

15	赞美	praise	16	忧愁	sad
18	柳树	willow	19	分离	separate
21	纯洁	pure			

17	特殊	special
20	红豆	red bean

Translation

❸ The wind, the flowers, the snow and the moon in the Chinese poems

Chinese people fervently love the Great Nature. Many Chinese poets have described and praised the Great Nature in their poems. In China there are a lot of landscape poems, which portray natural scenery of mountains, rivers, flowers and trees. There are also a lot of pastoral poems, which portray the rural scenery of the countryside. When you read these beautiful poems you will feel that you have entered the scenery portrayed in the poems.

Chinese poets use the method of portrayal of the scenery of Nature to express their feelings. In Chinese poems the scenery of Nature is personified like people. It can be happy and it can be sad. When the poet is happy even the wind in the poem is happy. When the poet is sad the flower in the poem also cries.

In Chinese poems the scenery of Nature frequently has special implications. For instance the moon in the poems frequently expresses how the poets miss their relatives, their friends or their home villages. When a poet cannot bear the sadness of the moment that he is separating from a friend he frequently uses the portrayal of the willow tree to express this feeling of the desire not to be separated. When a poet portrays that a plum blossom is not afraid of the cold he is praising the perseverance and the courage of the plum blossom and using this comparison to portray and to praise someone who is just as strong and as courageous as that plum blossom. In Western poems red roses are frequently used to express love. In Chinese poems red beans and peach blossom flowers are used for the portrayal of love. In Western poems lily flowers are used to represent purity. In Chinese poems lotus flowers are used for the same purpose, instead of the lily flowers.

An art village in today's China — The Beijing 798 Factory District

When you first get close to the Beijing 798 Factory District you may feel that they are like ordinary old factories. Tall chimneys and broken surrounding walls are everywhere. But when you look carefully you will discover a lot of posters, sculptures and art workshops. Also there are a lot of artists who have their special and individualistic styles. As a matter of fact this is not an ordinary old factory district but it is a famous art district in Beijing. It is like the Soho district in New York, the East End London and the Zimmer strasse in Berlin. This is the area where the artists express their art talents and exchange their ideas.

The 798 Factory was an industrial area in 1950s. In recent years the factories were being abandoned and left to rot. The owners were willing to rent out these factories at a very low rate. From the beginning of 2002 a lot of Chinese and overseas artists have been renting these factories as their workshops or opening up art galleries in these factories. Within a few years there are close to 100 art institutes being established here. Talented Chinese artists and collectors concentrate here. They work here and the live here and they create and display their works of art here. If you want to understand more about modern Chinese art please come to Beijing 798 Factory District and see for yourselves.

GAMES FOR FUN

In Chinese poems and paintings one can frequently see objects of the Great Nature like bamboo trees and pine trees etc. To Chinese people these objects have special implications. Do you know what do they represent and what are their meanings?

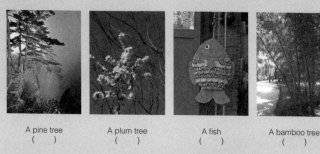

A pine tree   A plum tree   A fish   A bamboo tree
(   )   (   )   (   )   (   )

A. A.Someone is not afraid of difficulties / Longevity
B. Integrity
C. Strength, perseverance, pride and high self-esteem
D. Wealth, affluence and good fortune

Answers:

A C D B

A pine tree: Pine tree is evergreen tree and does not wither in the winter but it is straight and strong, so Chinese people think it can represent the spirit of perseverance and the strong will of not giving up easily. Besides, it is regarded as a symbol of longevity.

A bamboo tree: Chinese people use bamboo trees to symbolize integrity and humbleness as they are hallowed inside and very straight outside. And people with these qualities are regarded as gentlemen.

A plum blossom: Plum blossoms flower in the winter. Chinese people think that they can excel in such harsh conditions and blossom into flowers shows that they are different from other flowers and they have the qualities of a strong will and have high self-esteem with pride.

A fish: The Chinese pronunciation of both characters "鱼" or "a fish"and"余" or "leftover", are the same. "余yu" means the state of excess in affluence and "鱼yu" thus becomes the symbol of wealth and high social esteem. During Chinese New Year, people will prepare pictures of fishes at home and eat fishes to try to get the good omen of having annual excess.

Zhōngguórén chuān zěnyàng de yīfu

中国人穿怎样的衣服？

What Kinds of Clothes do Chinese People Wear?

Pre-reading Questions

1. Japanese people still wear their kimonos but do the Chinese still wear their traditional national dresses?

2. Let's check out the clothes and see whether there is any "Made in China" label.

3. Which European and American clothing name brands that you know of have opened up their designer shops in China?

Dàibiǎo Zhōngguó de fúzhuāng   qípáo hé zhōngshān zhuāng

❶ 代表 中国 的 服装 —— 旗袍 和 中山 装

Zhōngguó yǒu yōujiǔ[1] de lìshǐ dànshì xiànzài dàibiǎo

中国 有 悠久[1] 的 历史，但是 现在 代表

Zhōngguó de fúzhuāng qípáo hé zhōngshān zhuāng què shì

中国 的 服装 —— 旗袍 和 中山 装，却 是 20

shìjì cái chūxiàn de Qípáo shì nǚxìng chuān de jiǎncái

世纪 才 出现 的！旗袍 是 女性 穿 的，剪裁[2]

hěn jiǎngjiu jǐn tiē zhe shēntǐ Zài lóngzhòng chǎnghé chuān de

很 讲究[3]，紧 贴 着 身体。在 隆重[4] 场合[5] 穿 的

qípáo dàduōshù yòng sīchóu zuò chéng yào liáng shēn dìng zào

旗袍 大多数 用 丝绸 做成，要 量[6] 身 订造。

The Qipao worn by Empress Dowager, Cixi

Qípáo shang yòng jié zuò niǔkòu
旗袍 上 用 结 做 钮扣。

Dàn zuìchū de qípáo bìng bù
但 最初 的 旗袍 并 不

shì zhèyàng de
是 这样 的。

Qípáo běnlái shì Zhōngguó
旗袍 本来 是 中国

de yī gè shǎoshùmínzú
的 一 个 少数民族——

Mǎnzú de fúzhuāng Zuìchū de qípáo shì kuānsōng de cháng
满族 的 服装[7]。最初 的 旗袍 是 宽松[8] 的 长

páo Nǐ jiàn guo Cíxǐ tàihòu de zhàopiàn ma Tā chuān
袍。你 见 过 慈禧 太后 的 照片 吗？她 穿

de jiùshì qípáo Hòulái Mǎnzú jiànlì de Qīngcháo gōngyuán
的 就是 旗袍。后来，满族 建立 的 清朝（公元

nián zhì nián mièwáng le dànshì qípáo de
1616 年 至 1911 年）灭亡[9] 了，但是 旗袍 的

yǐngxiǎng méiyǒu xiāoshī Shànghǎi de fúzhuāng shèjì shī shòudào
影响 没有 消失。上海 的 服装 设计 师 受到

wàiguó fúshì de yǐngxiǎng bǎ qípáo biànchéng le jǐn shēn
外国 服饰[10] 的 影响，把 旗袍 变成 了 紧身[11]

de Cóng shí jiǔ shìjì èr shí niándài kāishǐ qípáo
的。从 十 九 世纪 二 十 年代 开始，旗袍

yīzhí shòudào Zhōngguó nǚxìng xǐ'ài
一直 受到 中国 女性 喜爱。

Zhōngguó nánxìng chuān shénme ne Zài Qīngdài
中国 男性 穿 什么 呢？在 清代，

tāmen chuān yòu kuān yòu dà chángdù dào jiǎo de cháng
他们 穿 又 宽 又 大，长度 到 脚 的 长

páo wàimian zài jiā yī jiàn shàngyī jiàozuò mǎguà
袍，外面 再 加 一 件 上衣，叫做 马褂。

Qīngcháo jiéshù hòu, Sūn Zhōngshān dāng shang
清朝 结束 后， 孙 中山 当 上

zǒngtǒng。 Tā zhǔchí[12] shèjì le yī tào
总统。 他 主持 设计 了 一 套

yīfu， zhè tào yīfu yòng le Sūn Zhōngshān
衣服， 这 套 衣服 用 了 "孙 中山"

de míngzi， jiàozuò zhōngshān zhuāng。 Zhōngshān zhuāng
的 名字， 叫做 中山 装。 中山 装

shàngyī yǒu sì gè dàizi， dàizi shang yǒu
上衣 有 四 个 袋子， 袋子 上 有

The Zhongshan Suit worn by Dr. Sun Yat-sen

gàizi hé niǔkòu， xiàshēn shì xīzhuāng cháng kù。 Zhōngshān zhuāng
盖子 和 钮扣， 下身 是 西装 长 裤。 中山 装

hěn kuài jiù zài Zhōngguó liúxíng， bìng chéngwéi Zhōngguó nánxìng de
很 快 就 在 中国 流行， 并 成为 中国 男性 的

zhèng zhuāng。 Bùguāng Sūn Zhōngshān chuān zhōngshān zhuāng， Máo Zédōng
正 装。 不光 孙 中山 穿 中山 装， 毛 泽东

hé Dèng Xiǎopíng yě chángcháng chuān Zhōngshān zhuāng。
和 邓 小平 也 常常 穿 中山 装。

GLOSSARY

1 悠久 long
2 剪裁 cutting
3 讲究 fastidious
4 隆重 grand
5 场合 occasion
6 量 measure
7 服装 costume
8 宽松 loose
9 灭亡 end; die
10 服饰 fashion; clothes and accessories
11 紧身 close-fitting
12 主持 take charge of

Translation

❶ The national dresses that represent China — the Qipao and the Zhongshan Suit

Although China has a long history, the national dresses that represent China today — the qipao and the Zhongshan Suit only made their first appearances in the 20th century. Qipaos are for ladies and the cutting is very fastidious, requiring them to be close-fitting to the body. Qipaos worn during important ceremonial occasions are usually made of silk and they have to be custom-made. The buttons used on qipaos are knots tied with fine bundles made from silk or other similar materials. But the original classical style of qipaos does not look like the modern version.

Originally the qipao was worn by ladies from a Chinese ethnic minority, the Manchurian (called Man, 满, in Chinese) Tribe, which had its own style of dress — this original version of the qipao was a loose-fitting long robe. Have you seen the picture of the Empress Dowager? The robe she was wearing in the picture is the original style of the qipao. Later on, the Qing Dynasty (1616 — 1911), established by the Manchurian Man Tribe ended but the influence of the qipao did not disappear. Being influenced and inspired by overseas fashion styles the fashion designers of Shanghai changed the qipao into its close–fitting look. Since the beginning of the second decade of the nineteenth century, the qipao has been very popular with Chinese ladies.

What do Chinese men wear then? In the Qing Dynasty men wore a long robe that extended to the feet. They were big and loose fitting. Over the long robe they wore a Mandarin jacket, called magua in Chinese. After the end of the Qing Dynasty Dr. Sun Zhongshan(Dr. Sun Yat-sen)became the president of China and he directed the design of a set of clothes, which was named after him as the Zhongshan Suit because he was called Sun Zhongshan. The Zhongshan Suit has four pockets, each of which has a pocket cover and a button. The lower half of the Zhongshan Suit is a pair of regular trousers of the Western suit. The Zhongshan Suit has become popular rapidly ever since and it is the national dress of a Chinese gentleman and has been regarded as formal enough clothing for important occasions. The Zhongshan Suit was not only worn by Dr. Sun Zhongshan, it was frequently worn by Chairman Mao Zedong and Mr. Deng Xiaoping.

❷ 中国 服饰 的 演变
Zhōngguó fúshì de yǎnbiàn

Chuántǒng Hànzú de yīfu chángcháng shì yī jiàn cháng páo
传统 汉族 的 衣服 常常 是 一件 长 袍，

huòzhě shàng xià fēnkāi de yīshang yòng sīchóu zuò chéng xiù
或者 上 下 分开 的 衣裳，用 丝绸 做 成，绣[13]

shang gèzhǒng tú'àn Zuì dà de tèdiǎn shì kuò páo dà xiù
上 各种 图案[14]。最 大 的 特点 是 阔 袍 大 袖。

Dàn qióngrén zhǐ néng chuān cūbù zuò chéng de duǎn yī cháng kù
但 穷人 只 能 穿 粗布 做 成 的 短 衣 长 裤。

Kuò páo dà xiù suīrán hěn piàoliang dànshì bù
阔 袍 大 袖 虽然 很 漂亮，但是 不

fāngbiàn yóuqí shì zuòzhàn de shíhou Zhōngguó běifāng de
方便，尤其 是 作战 的 时候。中国 北方 的

mínzú jīngcháng yào qí mǎ tāmen yīfu de tèdiǎn shì
民族 经常 要 骑 马，他们 衣服 的 特点 是

shàngyī shì zhǎi xiù xiàshēn shì kùzi Wèile zuòzhàn
上衣 是 窄[15] 袖，下身 是 裤子[16]。为了 作战

huòdé shènglì Hànzú céngjīng xué běifāng mínzú chuān zhǎi xiù
获得[17] 胜利，汉族 曾经 学 北方 民族 穿 窄 袖

yīfu hé kùzi Yī qiān wǔ bǎi nián qián
衣服 和 裤子。一 千 五 百 年 前，

běifāng de shǎoshùmínzú jìnrù chángchéng yǐnán
北方 的 少数民族 进入 长城 以南

jūzhù Bùtóng mínzú de fúzhuāng kāishǐ
居住。不同 民族 的 服装 开始

hùxiāng yǐngxiǎng Hànzú chuān qi shǎoshùmínzú
互相 影响。汉族 穿 起 少数民族

de kùzi shǎoshùmínzú de guìzú yě
的 裤子，少数民族 的 贵族 也

xǐhuan chuān Hànzú de fúshì
喜欢 穿 汉族 的 服饰。

The costume of the
ancient Han race

唐朝（公元 618 年至 907 年）的服饰还受到西方的影响。因为当时丝绸之路很畅通[18]，中亚和波斯[19]的服装很流行。

The costume in the Tang Dynasty

唐朝的女装领口[20]很低，披一条长巾，这是西方的穿衣方法。有时唐朝女子又穿男人的衣服。

到了清代，满族统治中国，汉族男性必须穿满族服饰，剃去前面的头发，在脑后梳[22]辫子[23]。汉族女性可以不穿满族服装。

The costume of a man in the Qing Dynasty

中国服饰在几千年的演变中，既有汉族的传统，又一直受到少数民族服饰和外来服饰的影响。

GLOSSARY

13	绣	embroider	14	图案	pattern
15	窄	narrow	16	裤子	pants
17	获得	gain	18	畅通	unblocked
19	波斯	Persia	20	领口	collar
21	剃	shave	22	梳	comb
23	辫子	plait			

Translation

❷ The evolution of the costume of the Chinese people

Traditionally the costume of the Han Chinese usually consisted of a long robe or a dress divided into a top half and a lower half. These robes and dresses were made of silk with all kinds of embroidery patterns on them. The special feature of this dress style was a loose-fitting robe with big sleeves. But the poor could only wear short robes with long pants made from cloth of coarse materials.

The style of a loose-fitting robe with big sleeves might look beautiful but wearing these clothes made it inconvenient to move around, especially in battles. The northern ethnic tribes of China frequently had to ride horses (as a form of transportation). The special feature of their clothes was a pair of narrow sleeves and they wore a pair of pants. In order to gain victory in battles the Han Chinese at one time imitated the dress style of the northern ethnic tribes. They wore clothes with narrow sleeves and they wore pants too. One thousand and five hundred years ago northern ethnic minorities entered into the region south of the Great Wall and made their homes there. Dress styles of different ethnic tribes began to influence one another. The Han Chinese began to wear pants like the ethnic minorities and the aristocrats of ethnic minorities also liked to dress up like the Han Chinese.

In the Tang Dynasty (618 — 907) the costume style was also subjected to Western influences made possible by the frequent and large volume of traffic along the Silk Road. At that time the dress styles of the Middle East and Persia were very popular. The collar of a lady's dress in the Tang Dynasty was very low, draped with a long stole (on the neck). That was the Western style of dressing up as ladies (not the Han style). Ladies of the Tang Dynasty also put on men's clothes.

In the Qing Dynasty, China was ruled by the Manchurian Man Tribe. Han Chinese men were ordered to dress up like male members of the Manchurian Tribe. The hair of the front part of the head must be shaved off completely and the long hair behind the head plaited into a braid of hair like a tail. Han ladies were exempt from the dress code order and they did not have to wear costumes of the Manchurian Man Tribe.

In the several thousand years of the evolution of the costume of China the style can be summed up as the style of the Han Chinese tradition, which has all the time been influenced by costume styles of ethnic minorities and foreign dress styles from the outside world.

❸ 今天 的 中国 服饰
Jīntiān de Zhōngguó fúshì

今天 中国人 平日 已 不 会 穿 传统 的
Jīntiān Zhōngguórén píngrì yǐ bù huì chuān chuántǒng de

服饰，穿 的 衣服 与 美国、欧洲、日本、韩国
fúshì chuān de yīfu yǔ Měiguó Ōuzhōu Rìběn Hánguó

等等 国家 的 人 一样，没有 什么 大 分别。
děngděng guójiā de rén yīyàng méiyǒu shénme dà fēnbié

The name brand apparel — specialty shops in China

男性 也 穿 西装²⁴，打 领带，穿 T 恤衫、牛仔裤、运动 鞋。背心²⁵、连衣 裙²⁶、超 短 裙²⁷也 出现 在 中国 女性 的 衣柜²⁸ 里。但 在 80 年代 之前，中国 大陆 的 服装 非常 单调²⁹。你 能 看 到 的 服装 大 部分 只有 蓝色、白色、绿色、灰色、黑色，只有 中山 装、衬衫、军装、长裤。在 八 十 年代 实行 开放 政策³⁰ 后，不少 商店 渐渐 也 开始 出售 国际 名牌³¹ 服装。例如 Nike, Adidas, Tommy, Hilfiger, Calvin, Klein 等 牌子 现在 在 中国 都 有 专门 店³²。中国人 很 欢迎 这些 名牌 的 服饰，以后 还 将 有 更 多 的 国际 名牌 进入 中国 市场。现在 中国 是 世界 上 最 大 的 服装 生产 国 之 一。事实上，很多 世界 名牌 的 服装 都 是 在 中国 制造 的。

现在，中国人 在 特别 的 日子 里，或者

在 隆重 的 场合 中 也 会
zài lóngzhòng de chǎnghé zhōng yě huì

穿 传统 服装。例如，过
chuān chuántǒng fúzhuāng Lìrú guò

春节 时 会 穿上 传统 的
chūnjié shí huì chuān shang chuántǒng de

民族 服装，自己 或 亲人
mínzú fúzhuāng zìjǐ huò qīnrén

结婚 时 汉族 的 人 会 穿
jiéhūn shí Hànzú de rén huì chuān

The traditional wedding costume of the Chinese

上 旗袍、龙凤褂³³；章 子怡 和 巩 俐 等 中国
shang qípáo lóngfèngguà Zhāng Zǐyí hé Gǒng Lì děng Zhōngguó

女 明星 都 曾 穿 旗袍 参加 国际 电影 活动。
nǚ míngxīng dōu céng chuān qípáo cānjiā guójì diànyǐng huódòng

GLOSSARY

24 西装　suit
25 背心　sleeveless jackets
26 连衣裙　frock-style dress
27 超短裙　mini-skirt
28 衣柜　wardrobe
29 单调　dull
30 政策　policy
31 名牌　famous brand
32 专门店　specialty shops
33 褂　Chinese-style wedding gowns

Translation

❸ The Costume Style of Today's China

Today in China ordinary people do not wear traditional costumes. The clothes they wear are the same as those worn in America, Europe, Japan and Korea. There are no big differences. Men wear Western style suits with neckties. They wear t-shirts and jeans. They wear running shoes too. Sleeveless jackets, frock-style dresses and even tiny mini-skirts are popular with Chinese women. Before the 80s the costume style in China was very monotonous. The clothes that you could see were colored in blue, white, green, grey and black. The costume style as a whole consisted only of the Zhongshan Suits, dress shirts, military uniforms and long trousers. In the 80s after the Open Policy was in practice quite a few stores gradually began to sell internationally known brand name clothing, like Nike, Adidas, Tommy Hilfiger, Calvin Klein, each of which has a chain of specialty shops in China now. Chinese people like and welcome these kinds of clothes and ornaments of the brand names. In the future there will be even more brand names entering the Chinese market. Now China is one of the largest clothing producers in the world and many of the products of these world-known brand names are made in China.

Now Chinese people may also wear their traditional costumes at special festivals or formal ceremonies. For example, during the Spring Festival of Chinese New Year Chinese ethnic minorities may wear their traditional costumes. At weddings the brides or their relatives may also wear qipaos or wedding gowns with dragon and phoenix embroidery. Chinese film stars like Zhang Ziyi and Gong Li usually wear qipaos when promoting their films to an international audience.

Hair braids: The Men's Hairstyle of the Manchurian Man Tribe

The ancient Han Chinese regarded cutting one's hair as an act showing disrespect to one's parents. So they never cut their hair. Since early days they had been tying up their long hair. Plaiting it into a braid was one of the hairstyles. A few thousand years ago in the Shang Dynasty there were already people tying up their hair into a braid. After the Qin Dynasty very few Han Chinese men wore a braid of hair.

The living habits of the northern ethnic minorities were different from that of the Han Chinese. They had the habit of shaving off the top part of their hair. After shaving off the top part of their hair they let the surrounding hair loosely hanging. Later on they plaited it into braids of hair for easier care. People of the Mongolian Tribe and the Manchurian Man Tribe also had this habit of plaiting their hair into hair braids.

In 1644 the Manchurian Man Tribe began to rule China and the Manchurian rulers forced the Han Chinese men to shave their heads and to braid their hair into the long pigtail style. From then on for over 200 years all Chinese men had a long braid of hair behind their heads. This long braid hairstyle of the Chinese men became their distinctive mark in appearance.

Up until 1911, in the year of the Xinhai Revolution, in which the Chinese bourgeois democratic revolution led by Dr. Sun Yat-sen overthrew the Qing Dynasty of the Manchurian Man Tribe the new Namjing Nationalist Government required Chinese men to cut off their braids of hair. From then on Chinese men's hairstyle has become like today's popular short hairstyle.

GAMES FOR FUN

Be a fashion designer for this one time! Please take a look and decide how you are going to match the dresses and the ornaments?

1. A Dragon-phoenix Gown
2. A Zhongshan Suit
3. A modern Qipao
4. A Qipao of the Qing Dynasty

A   B   C   D

Answers:
1-C 2-D 3-A 4-B

Guò yi guò Zhōngguó de jiérì

过一过中国的节日

Let's experience the festivals of China

Pre-reading Questions

1. Why are the golf ball shaped-and-sized rice dumplings and the moon cakes that Chinese people eat during festivals round in shape?

2. Why do Chinese people always spend time together with their families during the celebration of the Spring Festival?

3. How do the Chinese people celebrate the chinese Valentine's Day?

Zhōngguó de chuántǒng jiérì
❶ 中国 的 传统 节日

Zhōngguó rén yǒu hěn duō jiérì zhèxiē jiérì de
中 国 人 有 很 多 节 日， 这 些 节 日 的

rìzi zhǔyào shì yī nónglì lái jìsuàn de Yì nián zhōng
日 子 主 要 是 依 农 历 来 计 算 的。 一 年 中，

dì yī gè jiérì shì Chūnjié Gǔ shíhou Chūnjié yīzhí
第 一 个 节 日 是 春 节。 古 时 候 春 节 一 直

dào nónglì zhēngyuè shí wǔ Yuánxiāojié cái jiéshù Yuánxiāojié
到 农 历 正 月¹ 十 五 元 宵 节 才 结 束， 元 宵 节

yě shì Zhōngguó de Qíngrénjié Zhè shì yī nián zhōng dì yī
也 是 中 国 的 情 人 节。 这 是 一 年 中 第 一

A moon cake

gè yuè yuán de rìzi,
个 月 圆 的 日子，

yījiārén huì yīqǐ chī
一家人 会 一起 吃

tāngyuán dàibiǎo yījiā
汤圆[2]， 代表 一家

tuányuán Wǎnshang hái huì diǎn
团圆。晚上 还 会 点

qi hěn duō huādēng Dào nónglì sān yuè zuǒyòu yǒu jìbài
起 很 多 花灯。到 农历 三 月 左右，有 祭拜[3]

zǔxiān de Qīngmíngjié Zhè shíhou jīngcháng xià xiǎo yǔ
祖先 的 清明节。这 时候 经常 下 小 雨。

Dàjiā dào jiāowài sǎo mù huáiniàn xiānrén Jiē xialai de
大家 到 郊外[4] 扫墓[5]，怀念[6] 先人。接 下来 的

shì nónglì wǔ yuè wǔ rì de Duānwǔjié Duānwǔjié shì
是 农历 五 月 五 日 的 端午节。端午节 是

wèile jìniàn èrqiānduōnián qián zhùmíng de shīrén Qū Yuán
为了 纪念[7] 二千多年 前 著名 的 诗人 屈原。

Tā shì yī gè zhōngchéng de hǎo guānyuán dàn dāngshí de
他 是 一 个 忠诚[8] 的 好 官员，但 当时 的

guówáng què bù xiāngxìn tā tā dàochù liúlàng xiě le hěn
国王 却 不 相信 他，他 到处 流浪[9]，写 了 很

duō shī Zài wǔ yuè chūwǔ zhè tiān tā tiàojiāng zìshā
多 诗。在 五 月 初五 这 天，他 跳江 自杀，

dāngnián dàjiā qiāo dǎ luógǔ
当年 大家 敲 打 锣鼓[10]、

zài jiāng shang huá lóngchuán yòu
在 江 上 划 龙船，又

zuò yī zhǒng jiàozuò zòngzi
做 一 种 叫做 "粽子[11]"

de shíwù rēng jìn jiāng li
的 食物 扔 进 江 里，

Rice Dumplings

134

希望 鱼 儿 吃 饱
粽子 以后，不 会
吃 屈 原 的 身体。
现在 大家 也 划
龙船，也 做 粽子，

Rice dumplings wrapped up in bamboo leaves

但 粽子 留 着 自己 吃。到了 农历 八 月
十 五，就是 中秋节。这 一 天 月亮 最 圆，
也 是 家人 团聚[12] 的 日子。全 家 会 一起
赏月 和 吃 月饼。月饼 也 和 汤圆 一样 是
圆 的，也 代表 团圆。农历 九 月 初九 是
重阳节，这 天 大 家 会 去 爬山，叫做 登高。
从前 登高 是 为了 避 瘟疫[13]，现在 大家 当作
做 运动。冬至 在 农历 十二月，也是 非常 受
重视 的 节日。在 这 天 北方 人 会 吃 饺子，
南方 人 会 吃 汤圆。这 种 传统 一直 保留
到 今天。

GLOSSARY

1 正月 the first lunar calendar month
2 汤圆 golf ball sized-and-shaped rice dumplings with stuffing inside
3 祭拜 worship ancestors   4 郊外 countryside
5 扫墓 visit the graves of one's ancestors
6 怀念 in memory of someone   7 纪念 commemorate
8 忠诚 loyal   9 流浪 wandering
10 锣鼓 gong and drum
11 粽子 rice dumplings usually in a pyramid shape
12 团聚 reunite   13 瘟疫 plague; pestilence

Translation

❶ The traditional festivals of China

Chinese people have a lot of festivals. On what days to celebrate these festivals are mainly calculated according to the Chinese lunar calendar. Within one year the first festival is the Spring Festival. In ancient China, the Spring Festival lasted till the 15th of the first lunar calendar month, when it was the Yuanxiao Festival, the night of the 15th of the first full moon of the year. The Yuanxiao Festival marked the end of the Spring Festival and it was and still is the Chinese version of Valentine's Day. Since it is the first full moon of the year members of the whole family will gather together to eat golf ball sized-and-shaped rice dumplings with stuffing inside, symbolizing the happy family union together. During the night a lot of lanterns will be lighted up. When it is about the third lunar month of the Chinese calendar year there is another festival, called the Qingming Festival, when people worship their ancestors. During this period of the year it usually rains lightly and people go to the countryside to visit the graves of their ancestors in memory of their ancestors. The next festival is the Duanwu Festival in the fifth month of the Chinese lunar calendar. The Duanwu Festival is commemorates a famous poet, Qu Yuan, who lived over 2000 years ago. He was an loyal and good government officer but the king at that time did not trust him. He ended up wandering everywhere and composed a lot of poems. On the fifth day of the fifth month of the Chinese lunar calendar he committed suicide by jumping into the river. During that time people beat the gongs and the drums and rowed dragon boats on the river. They also made a certain kind of food, called "Zhongzis" (rice dumplings) and threw them into the river hoping the fish would eat that to their hearts' content and become so full that they would leave the body of Qu Yuan alone. Now people still row the dragon boats and they still make those rice dumplings. But instead of throwing them into the river they eat those rice dumplings themselves. Then on the 15th of the eighth month of the Chinese lunar calendar it is the Mid-autumn Festival. On that day the full moon is supposed to be the fullest in a circular shape. It is also the day of family gathering together. The whole family will get together to appreciate the beauty of the full moon and to eat moon cakes. Like the golf ball shaped-and-sized rice dumplings moon cakes are also round in shape, symbolizing a complete union. On the ninth day of the ninth month of the Chinese lunar calendar it is the Chongyang festival. On that day people will climb up the mountain, an activity, called denggao (登高). In ancient China people climbed up the high mountain in order to avoid the plague too. Now people do that for exercise. In the 12th month of the Chinese lunar calendar it is the celebration of the winter solstice, northern Chinese will eat substantial stuffed dumplings and southern Chinese will eat golf ball sized-and-shaped rice dumplings. This tradition has been kept till today.

❷ 最重要的节日——春节
Zuì zhòngyào de jiérì　　Chūnjié

Zhōngguó de jiérì hái yǒu hěn duō. Zhème duō
中国 的 节日 还 有 很 多。这么 多
de jiérì zhōng Chūnjié shì zuì zhòngyào zuì rè'nao de
的 节日 中,春节 是 最 重要、最 热闹[14] 的。
Érqiě Zhōngguó de jiātíng dōu huì yījiārén tuánjù zài
而且 中国 的 家庭 都 会 一家人 团聚 在
yìqǐ dùguò zhège Chūnjié jiàqī Chūnjié cóng nónglì
一起,度过 这个 春节 假期。春节 从 农历
zhēngyuè chūyī kāishǐ Zhòngshì nóngyè de gǔdài Zhōngguórén
正月 初一 开始。重视 农业 的 古代 中国人
zài zhège shíhou qìngzhù dōngtiān guòqu bìng qíqiú xīn yī
在 这个 时候 庆祝 冬天 过去,并 祈求[15] 新 一
nián fēngshōu suǒyǐ Chūnjié yě jiào guònián Chūnjié qián
年 丰收[16],所以 春节 也 叫"过年"。春节 前
de bàn gè yuè huǒchē zhàn qìchē zhàn fēijī chǎng biàn
的 半个 月,火车 站、汽车 站、飞机 场 便

The firework

jǐ mǎn le jí zhe huíjiā de
挤 满 了 急着 回家 的
rén Chūnjié qián fángzi bìdìng
人。春节 前,房子 必定
yào dǎsǎo gānjìng ránhòu zài
要 打扫 干净,然后 在
mén shang tiē xīnnián zhùfú yǔ
门 上 贴 新年 祝福 语[17],
yě jiùshì duìlián Chúxī
也 就是"对联[18]"。除夕
yè quánjiā rén yìqǐ chīfàn
夜,全家 人 一起 吃饭,
jiào chúxī fàn yě jiào
叫"除夕 饭",也 叫

People go back home to have a year-end family gathering dinner

tuánniánfàn　Xīnnián　de
"团年饭"。新年 的

zhōng shēng qiāo xiǎng yǐhòu
钟 声 敲 响 以后，

jiēshang de pàozhú shēng jiù
街上 的 炮竹[19] 声 就

xiǎng qi Chūyī dàjiā
响 起。初一，大家

chuān zhe piàoliang de yīfu gěi zhǎngbèi bàinián gěi xiǎohái
穿 着 漂亮 的 衣服，给 长辈 拜年，给 小孩

hóng bāo Chū'èr kāishǐ bàifǎng qīnrén péngyou zhùhè
"红 包[20]"。初二 开始，拜访[21] 亲人 朋友，祝贺

xīnnián Chūnjié qījiān hěn duō dìfang yǒu wǔshī
新年。春节 期间，很 多 地方 有 舞狮、

yóu huāshì guàng miàohuì děng huódòng dàochù dōu hěn
游 花市、逛 庙会[22] 等 活动，到处 都 很

rè'nao yīzhí dào zhēngyuè shí wǔ de
热闹，一直 到 正月 十 五 的

Yuánxiāojié Xiànzài dūshì shēnghuó hěn
元宵节。现在，都市 生活 很

mánglù hěn duō rén Chūnjié zhǐ xiǎngyǒu
忙碌[23]，很 多 人 春节 只 享有

jǐ tiān de jiàqī jiérì qìfēn yě
几 天 的 假期，节日 气氛[24] 也

méiyǒu yǐqián nàme nóng
没有 以前 那么 浓。

The lion dance that celebrate the lunar Chinese new year

GLOSSARY

14 热闹 boisterous
16 丰收 an abundant harvest
18 对联 couplets
20 红包 lucky money
22 庙会 temple visitation
24 气氛 atmosphere

15 祈求 pray for
17 祝福语 blessing
19 炮竹 firecracker
21 拜访 pay a visit
23 忙碌 busy

Translation

❷ The most important festival-the Spring Festival

China has a lot more other festivals. Among all these numerous festivals the most important and boisterous is the Spring Festival. Chinese families will get together and spend time as a family during the Spring Festival, which starts on the first day of the first month of the Chinese lunar calendar. In ancient times, when people placed a high significance on agriculture this was the festival celebrating the passing of winter and people wished to have an agriculturally abundant new year. Therefore the Spring Festival is also called "guonian, 过年, meaning the passing of the year". Half a month before the Spring Festival the train stations, the bus stations and the airports are crowded with a lot of people who are trying to rush home. Before the Spring Festival the house must be cleaned up completely and then "couplets" expressing New Year well wishes are put up on the door. On the eve of the Spring Festival all members of the family will get together to eat dinner, which is called "chuxifan, 除夕饭, meaning the new year eve dinner" or "tuannianfan, 团年饭, meaning the celebration of a complete family and a complete year dinner." When the midnight bell rings to signal the beginning of the new year the sound of fire crackers can be heard on the streets when people celebrate. On the first day of the New Year everyone dresses up beautifully and goes to visit senior members of the family. They called this "bainian" (拜年), literally meaning worshipping the year. Small children will be given the gift of "hongbao" (红包), or red pocket which has money inside. When the second day begins people go to visit their relatives and friends and congratulate one another on the arrival of the New Year. During the Spring Festival many places have activities like lion dances and flowers markets and temple visitations. It is hustle and bustle everywhere until the 15th day of the month, the celebration of the Yuanxiao Festival. Now the lifestyle of city people is very busy. Many people only have a few days of holidays for the Spring Festival. The mood of festivities is not as keen as before.

❸ 今天 的 中国 节日
Jīntiān de Zhōngguó jiérì

今天，中国 的 节日 发生 了 不少 变化。
Jīntiān Zhōngguó de jiérì fāshēng le bùshǎo biànhuà

有些 节日 逐渐 被 忘记，比如 七 月 初七 的
Yǒuxiē jiérì zhújiàn bèi wàngjì bǐrú qī yuè chūqī de

乞巧 节，古 时 妇女 会 在 这 一 天 比赛 针
Qǐqiǎo jié gǔ shí fùnǚ huì zài zhè yī tiān bǐsài zhēn

线 25 手工艺 26，现在 已 很 少 见；有些 庆祝
xiàn shǒugōngyì xiànzài yǐ hěn shǎo jiàn yǒuxiē qìngzhù

形式 则 有 了 变化，比如 元宵节，古 时 只
xíngshì zé yǒu le biànhuà bǐrú Yuánxiāojié gǔ shí zhǐ

是 看 花灯，如今 大陆 往往 还 会 放 烟花
shì kàn huādēng rújīn dàlù wǎngwǎng hái huì fàng yānhuā

庆祝。而 在 台湾，元宵节 的 花灯 会 仍然
qìngzhù Ér zài Táiwān Yuánxiāojié de huādēng huì réngrán

年 年 都 有。而且 还 有 大型 的 灯谜 会 和
nián nián dōu yǒu Érqiě hái yǒu dàxíng de dēngmí huì hé

花灯 夜市，有 很 多 人 去 观赏 和 游玩，
huādēng yèshì yǒu hěn duō rén qù guānshǎng hé yóuwán

非常 热闹。今天，很 多 节日 礼物 成 了
fēicháng rè'nao Jīntiān hěn duō jiérì lǐwù chéng le

商品，人们 不 再 需要 亲自 动手 做，在 商店
shāngpǐn rénmen bù zài xūyào qīnzì dòngshǒu zuò zài shāngdiàn

或 市场 就 能 轻易 买 到，有的 甚至 成为
huò shìchǎng jiù néng qīngyì mǎi dào yǒude shènzhì chéngwéi

中国 出口 产品，比如 月饼、粽子、花灯 等。
Zhōngguó chūkǒu chǎnpǐn bǐrú yuèbing zòngzi huādēng děng

现在 中国 还 多 了 不少 新 的 节日，这些
Xiànzài Zhōngguó hái duō le bùshǎo xīn de jiérì zhèxiē

节日 主要 是 来自 西方。比如 情人节 和
jiérì zhǔyào shì láizì xīfāng Bǐrú Qíngrénjié hé

The Lantern Festival of the first full moon of the New Year

Shèngdànjié   zuì   shòu   niánqīng   rén   huānyíng   le   Zài   zhèxiē
圣诞节，最　受　年轻　人　欢迎　了。在　这些

jiérì   li   niánqīng   rén   huì   gòumǎi   lǐwù   sòng   gěi   àiren
节日　里，年轻　人　会　购买　礼物　送　给　爱人。

Tāmen   hái   huì   hé   hǎo
他们　还　会　和　好

péngyou   yīqǐ   guàngjiē   qù
朋友　一起　逛街，去

chànggē   dào   jiǔbā
KTV 唱歌，到　酒吧

chàng   yǐn   cānjiā   gèzhǒng
畅　饮27，参加　各种

qìngzhù   huódòng   dùguò   yī
庆祝　活动，度过　一

gè   huānlè   de   wǎnshang
个　欢乐　的　晚上。

The street scene of Christmas in China

GLOSSARY

25 针线　needlework
27 畅饮　drink freely

26 手工艺　handicraft

Translation

❸ The festivals of today's China

Today festivals in China have undergone many changes. Some festivals are being gradually forgotten. For instance the Qiqiao (meaning begging skillfulness) Festival on the seventh day of the seventh month of the Chinese lunar calendar is not celebrated anymore. In ancient times, ladies on that day would compete with one another to see who was the best in the skill of needle embroidery art. It is seldom seen now. Some festivals have changed the forms of celebration. For instance, during the Yuanxiao Festival in ancient times people only appreciated the beauty of lanterns. Now in Mainland China there are usually firework displays for celebration. In Taiwan every year during the Yuanxiao Festival there are still many flower lantern meetings and there are still some large scale riddles written on lanterns and riddle-guessing gatherings and night market for flower lanterns. Many people go to watch and participate in these activities. It is very boisterous. Now many gifts for festival celebration have become commercial products. People do not have to make them anymore. They can easily buy these in store or markets. Some have even become export products of China, like moon cakes, rice dumplings, and flower lanterns etc. Now in China there are many more new festivals, which mainly came from the West. For example the celebration of Valentine's Day and the celebration of Christmas are two of the most popular among young people. During these festivals young people will buy gifts to send to their lovers and they will roam the streets together with their friends. They will go to ktv to sing and go to bars to drink to their hearts' content and participate in all kinds of activities of celebration to enjoy a happy night out.

The Chinese version of Valentine's Day

Please do not think that only in the West people enjoy their sweet Valentine's Day celebration. Chinese people too have a romantic festival similar to the celebration of Valentine's Day! It is the Yuanxiao Festival on the 15th of the first month of the Chinese lunar calendar. The Yuanxiao festival is also called the Lantern Festival. On this day people like to light up flower lanterns and now has developed into lantern meetings and riddles on lantern for riddle guessing. In ancient times, young girls could not go out easily without any reason. But on the night of the Yuanxiao Festival they could go out to appreciate lanterns. On that night young men and young ladies could get to know one another. On that day many beautiful and romantic stories have happened. Gradually the Yuanxiao Festival has become the romantic festival when young men and young ladies see each other and lovers meet each other. It has been called the "Chinese Valentine's Day". The Yuanxiao Festival of today is the same romantic festival as before. On the 15th day of the first month of the Chinese lunar calendar there are always a lot of bright light decorations everywhere on the streets. Just as on the streets of the celebration of Valentine's Day in the West some places in Mainland China have more activities than lantern meetings. People celebrate with firework displays. Lovers like to watch the display of firework while holding hands.

In Hong Kong people like Valentine s Day more than the Yuanxiao Festival. Whether in Mainland China, Taiwan, Hong Kong or overseas where there is a large population of Chinese people whenever there is a time when the Chinese Yuanxiao Festival and the celebration of Valentine's Day are close to each other then the romantic mood of festivities will continue for quite a few days.

GAMES FOR FUN

You can follow the suggestions below to fold up the paper into a small lantern. Then try to use Chinese patterns to decorate this lantern!

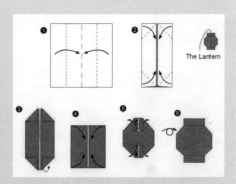

The Lantern